PRAISE FOR

COMATOSE MANAGEMENT

Six Short Stories of Destructive Management Practices

Through simple but effective and engaging stories, Sheaffer shows how bad management landed corporate America in its current financial predicament. "Comatose Management" illuminates basic truths that most of us prefer to ignore throughout our careers—preferring to believe our managers are brilliant but eccentric rather than overindulged, ego-maniacal, psychotic, or just plain clueless. Here's a wake-up call for all companies—and all employees at every level.

— Lorri Freifeld, Editor-in-Chief, Training and Sales & Marketing Management magazines

In "Comatose Management," Scott Sheaffer has created workplace narratives that sharply remind us of the "real world" of work and prepare us to create a work environment in which we don't just survive, but thrive. This book will wake you up and make you want to change something – your job, your way of thinking, your attitude.

> — Pauline Shirley, President, LeadersOnFire, Partner/Principal, Entrepreneur Leadership Center, Past International President, Toastmasters International

Scott's experience has given him keen insight into the interesting and unfortunate situations that managers often, inadvertently, create. This is a brilliant series of short stories that depict what managers do, every day, to get in the way of their own success. The stories relate how the manager's behavior and decisions are extremely pivotal in obtaining results in any organization – and an uneasy reminder of how all of us can be most careless with other people's careers. I recommend this stirring little read. It packs a punch.

> — Sue Miller, President, Sue Miller Training and Consulting

Experience is the best teacher and the master of all traits. "Comatose Management" brings to its readers the real life trials and tribulations of corporate employees and how you, whether in management or not, can survive and succeed. Thank you, Scott, for incorporating so many real life examples.

> — Janet Sue Rush, President, The Rush Company, international speaker and author of nine books including "Zig Ziglar Presents...Janet Rush on - Customer Service."

COMATOSE MANAGEMENT

Six Short Stories of Destructive
Management Practices

Scott R. Sheaffer

Copyright © 2009 Scott R. Sheaffer
All rights reserved.

ISBN: 1-4392-5103-7
ISBN-13: 9781439251034

Visit www.booksurge.com to order additional copies.

⌘ ⌘ ⌘

This book is dedicated to Bestemor
who always believed in me no matter what.

⌘ ⌘ ⌘

While these are fictionalized stories, they are all drawn in part from people and events I have observed. Any character depicted in this book who resembles a real person, whether living or deceased, is purely coincidental and unintended. Any company portrayed in this book that appears similar to an existing company, or one that is no longer in business, is completely accidental and unplanned.

Table of Contents

Introduction
vii

There Is No Plan
1

Empowered Imposters
27

The Productive Employee
53

Captain Nepotism
77

Only a Man Can Manage
99

Management by Emotion
123

INTRODUCTION

⌘ ⌘ ⌘

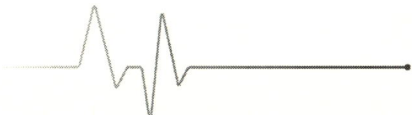

My friend, Zack, and I have been meeting every Saturday for coffee at the same Starbucks ever since we met at a seminar a few months ago. At these meetings Zack has voiced questions about various management and career issues. I've told him several stories based on my experiences and he found them helpful. Perhaps you will too. I have selected six of my favorites for this book.

Zack is a capable, knowledgeable and energetic sales manager. He is optimistic and enjoys working with people. People like working for Zack and he has no problem finding internal candidates for open positions because of the high regard his fellow employees have for him. He is representative of anyone who is responsible for

Comatose Management

making decisions that affect customers, probably not unlike your situation. He works for a mid-size manufacturer that has been in business for about 20 years. They are a privately owned company but plan to go public within the next two years. He has been with his current employer for almost three years but has worked for several other companies in his career. He has been promoted at each of his jobs. He is always seeking more challenges and has accepted offers from new employers when he feels that doing so would further his career. He is motivated by money but is primarily motivated by challenge and personal reward. Zack does not like office politics very much nor is he particularly skilled at handling political situations. He comes from the old school that teaches hard work, ability and a willingness to work as a team will get you ahead. For the most part, his old school formula has worked for Zack.

Zack is perplexed where he is currently working because he sees the company take ten steps forward and nine steps back…ten steps forward and nine steps back…ten steps forward and nine steps back. He has noticed that the nine steps back are frequently the same nine steps. He wonders why no one seems to be able to stop this insanity. The solutions seem obvious based on

Introduction

his experience. He wonders why these setbacks and disappointments continue year after year. He is frustrated that some of the executives of the company seem to lay the groundwork for some of these failures. Zack is optimistic that the stories I am telling him will shed light on some of the reasons for the inconsistent and incongruent behaviors he observes daily.

I told Zack there is really no advantage I can see for myself in getting older, other than gaining wisdom. What a price to pay for insight. I noticed many things in the workplace when I was young that didn't seem to make sense to me either. It appeared that sometimes the companies were purposely trying to hurt themselves. I could not adequately identify what was causing some of these problems because I had just graduated from college and had little experience. I naively believed that everyone knew more than I did and there was a master plan for everything. *Surely* the people in management knew what they were doing and could be trusted. *Obviously,* they had laid out careful plans. I reasoned that even if management were making decisions that *appeared* to be counter-productive or dysfunctional, they were still doing the right thing. I knew I didn't fully understand things. I later found that sometimes what appeared to be foolish decisions by management

Comatose Management

were the right decisions. At other times, I found this not to be the case.

I am embarrassed to admit that my insights about companies and how they are managed did not change significantly until I was much older. I had been working for almost twenty years by then. Two things transpired at that time to change my outlook on the business world forever.

The first event was going to work for a very well known Fortune 500 company in a sales management position. I really thought I had hit the jackpot. I had actually landed a management position in a very prominent corporation and I was going to learn *advanced management skills.* I had arrived. This company had thousands upon thousands of employees at the time and I was intimidated by every one of them, even though I had been brought in as a Director of Sales for one of their divisions. For my first few months I observed what looked like some bad decisions being made by management, just as I had observed in the smaller companies where I had worked previously. I could not understand why management appeared to be pursuing agendas that seemed to contradict the organization's goals. Just as I had always done, I found myself increasingly relying on the belief that this mega-corporation had the best and brightest

Introduction

in management and they were much more knowledgeable than I was. Clearly, they had well thought out strategies with supporting tactics. It must have been that I just was not capable of understanding.

The second event that played a role in my changing view of the business world was not an event as much as an awakening. I realized that I was seeing the same things in this giant corporation as I had seen in companies that had 100 employees. Many of the same things. This kind of counter-productive behavior was universal and appeared to be independent of company size. What was going on here? Do many, if not most, companies operate like this? I also was beginning to realize that I was not as ignorant or incompetent as I had previously feared. I found that I actually had learned a thing or two in my 40 years and realized that management was not always making *brilliant* decisions; in many cases, they were making uninformed and poor decisions. I found this to be equally true at both small companies and giant Fortune 500 companies. Management was just as capable of making atrocious decisions as were the receptionist and the janitor. People are people. The problem is that management's bad decisions cause more damage and affect more people. Furthermore, I awakened to the fact that

Comatose Management

there was no plan. Employees are caught in the misconception that everyone is operating under some grand strategy, but the reality is that there *is* no real strategy. Everyone was just reacting to events. I had been rationalizing peoples' behavior in order for things to make sense to me.

Of course, everybody makes mistakes. We are all human. I am not talking about mistakes and failures brought on by bad luck or intelligent risks that do not pay off. There will always be garden-variety problems that are a part of doing business. The kinds of bad decisions I am talking about are those you would expect to be obvious to management, but are not. Three well-known automotive product examples that come to mind are the Ford Edsel, Pontiac Aztec and Cadillac Cimarron. These cars made absolutely no sense and were notorious market failures for reasons that should have been apparent to everyone before they got off the drawing board. It's hard to believe no one in management stepped in to stop these obvious fiascos. I hope to provide some insight into some of the reasons things like this happen.

Why do so many managers make bad decisions on a continuing basis? Why is corporate planning done as an obligatory and perfunctory exercise? Why are incompetent people put in important positions? Why are they kept in those positions?

Introduction

Why do their subordinates act like nothing is askew? Why don't CEO's and Presidents recognize the dysfunctional behavior of their subordinates and do something about it (if they are not participating themselves)?

The reasons organizations, both big and small, are loaded with incompetent management and seem to continuously make poor business decisions are a result of beliefs we hold that go unquestioned or unrecognized. If we take a moment and actually think about what we are doing and why we are doing it, we begin to realize our behaviors and beliefs are frequently causing exactly the opposite outcome of what we desire. In this book I am going to present six short stories that represent examples of these behaviors.

You will see all the companies you have ever worked for in these stories. It is my hope that your conscious awareness will be jogged in a way that will enable you to make changes in yourself and your organization. I'm hoping this awareness will provide a competitive advantage for you and your company.

While these are fictionalized stories, they are all drawn in part from people and events I have observed. Any character depicted in this book who resembles a real person, whether living or deceased, is purely coincidental and unintended.

Comatose Management

Any company portrayed in this book that appears similar to an existing company, or one that is no longer in business, is completely accidental and unplanned.

1
THERE IS NO PLAN

⌘ ⌘ ⌘

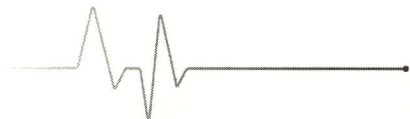

Zack called me recently, wanting to meet. He always seems to enjoy listening to my stories. We have always met at Starbucks, but for some reason he asked where we should meet this time. To my surprise Zack asked, "Where do you want to meet? We need to alter our plan a little to keep things fresh." I was a little surprised he would consider another place. To be honest, the thought of meeting at another place somewhat threw me off balance. Have I gotten this set in my ways?

I told him, "Zack, you are right; we do need to change our regular plan. Why don't we meet at Denny's and have breakfast in addition to drinking coffee?" He was receptive to the idea and we worked out the details. When I hung up the phone, I realized this was the first time I had ever thought of our meetings as a planned event. I thought they just happened. I didn't think we were operating under any kind of plan. This small change of plans made me realize what I wanted to talk about with Zack when we met at Denny's.

Zack and I were comfortably seated with our coffee. This was a booth that had seen some use. I charitably selected the bench with the duct tape repairs. "Changing our normal plans and selecting a new venue for our meeting made me think of a story I need to tell you, Zack. People and companies are funny when it comes to the word 'plan.' No two people think of it in the same way. Some people believe everyone else has a plan but them. Others believe they are the only ones who have a plan. There are those who think everyone has a plan, and finally there are still others who think absolutely no one is operating under a plan. These differing viewpoints on planning can have a dramatic impact on how businesses run, or *think* they are running." Zack's interest began to pique. He had never thought of all those possibilities and how they might influence how companies operate and how people view their jobs.

"I know you have a real-world story for me about this. Let's hear it."

There is No Plan

I began.

Sales were not good at Rubix Adhesives. Sales levels had barely been maintained over the last five years and the CEO of the company was getting increasingly concerned. His name was Rex Bolden. Their competitors' sales had increased an average of 12% per year during this same time-period. Rubix Adhesives was a $1.1 billion distributor of adhesives and seemed stuck on that number. Their supplier complement included all the major name brands and three private label brands. They had warehouses in seven different countries. Their stock was publicly traded. Rex had hired Don Staton as their VP of Sales three years ago, hoping he would turn things around. Nothing had changed though. Sales levels were almost exactly what they were when Don was hired and the same level they were five years ago. The Board of Directors had informed Rex that the stockholders were tired of waiting for revenue growth. Rex knew this meant his job was on the line. He was about to lose a $400,000 per year job that also included significant executive benefits. Something had to change for the better, and soon, or he would be out of a job.

Rex, as CEO, knew that ultimately he would have to be the person who made the changes that were needed to improve sales. He had known Don

Comatose Management

Staton, Rubix's VP of Sales, as a fellow member of Northwest Community Church for almost 20 years. Don had 15 years of sales management experience at a Fortune 500 pharmaceutical company. While there, he had been promoted to Southern Regional Executive Vice President of Hospital and Clinic New Business Development. Rex had heard many good things about Don and liked him. He knew he wanted him to lead Rubix's struggling sales efforts. Don also had an MBA from MIT's Sloan School of Business. Rex will never forget how impressed he was with Don's personal appearance the first time he met him. He had the handsomeness of an old-fashioned movie star and was dressed in what looked like a very expensive designer suit. Rex thought his verbal skills were outstanding too. Don had an air of hubris about him, but this should be expected from anyone of this quality, Rex thought. This was the new blood that Rubix needed. Rex had a good feeling about Don.

With the executive presence Don exuded and his vast amount of Fortune 500 experience, it was obvious to Rex that he needed to get Don on board. That was exactly what he did. He demoted the current Executive Director of Sales and brought Don in as the VP of Sales. Rex was surprised how much he had to pay Don to get him away from his Fortune 500 job at the pharmaceutical company. Don also wanted a great deal of executive level benefits that even went beyond what Rex had. The Board quickly approved the salary and benefits. They had already seen two years of flat sales and did not want to continue that trend.

Rex was a gentle soul on the outside but those who knew him well knew he had a temper. Despite showing his temper on frequent occasions to the other executives, he never once lost his cool with Don, even after three years of disappointing sales. The fact that Don was still at Rubix amazed most everyone because of Don's poor results. It appeared that Rex was giving Don special treatment for some reason. Most people thought of Rex as being extremely intelligent and were betting he knew exactly what he was doing when it came to Don. As one can imagine there was also wild speculation among some in the office as to why Don was still with Rubix and why the CEO appeared to give him preferential treatment. Theories ranged from ridiculous to realistic. One of the not-too-probable theories was that they both had some scheme working where they were stealing money from the company and were going to milk it as long as they could. Another silly theory was that Don had discovered some highly incriminating criminal background information about Rex. There were other crazy ideas as well but most of the employees dismissed them as unrealistic.

Most of the rank-and-file employees accepted that they did not have all of the information and trusted their CEO to be taking the correct course of action with Don, and sales in general. They believed that Rex had everyone's best interest at heart. However, there was a small group in management who had other ideas as to why Rex continued to hang on to Don despite frequent stockholder protestations and poor performance. These individuals had the benefit of additional information the rank-and-file did not have. They were in management and closer to Rex. Their insights had to be taken more seriously. Obviously, something was askew *somewhere* at Rubix. There were three management theories as to why Don continued to hold the top sales position despite the fact that Rubix was chronically in the sales doldrums.

Theory one. Rex had made several bad executive hires in his tenure as CEO and was hesitant to fire Don because it would be an admission of another bad hire. The VP of Marketing was the standout bad hire. She was incompetent from the get-go and everyone knew it. Rex became overly friendly with her, which made it almost impossible for him to give her any corrective input. There were rumors that there was a sexual component to the relationship. In reality, there probably were some shenanigans going on between the two of them that Mrs. Rex Bolden would not have appreciated. Fortunately, for Rex, she voluntarily quit after only about nine months on the job. The VP of Marketing notwithstanding, this theory did not hold too much weight because Rex had also made some good hires as well. Overall, his hiring record was no worse than most other CEO's. There were really no glaring red flags here.

Theory two. Don offered a lot in the way of executive presence, but very little in substance. It was almost as if he were only playing the *role* of VP of Sales. All show and no go. However, there was one thing Don did bring to the table for Rex – connections. In an irony that could only be created in corporate America, Rex had become dependent on Don. Don's poor performance over the last three years had been a major contributor to the peril Rex now faced with the Board. Don, however, was very well connected with many Fortune 500 companies and could probably help Rex find another CEO position if the Board decided to boot Rex. Simply stated, Rex did not want to alienate Don. He might need him in the near future. The very person who got him in this mess was the one who could save him too. Rex was hanging on to a sinking ship, thinking he might need the lifeboats later. While an intriguing theory, this one had to be discounted because, without question and true to his character, Don was going to take care of himself if Rex was fired, or if both of them were fired. In reality, Don would not make any effort to help Rex. It was also felt that Don, being incredibly arrogant, perceived his connections within these Fortune 500 companies to be substantially more significant than they really were. The sinking ship's lifeboats probably had holes in them.

Theory three. Don's sister was a clinical psychologist. She used her married name in her profession, Dr. Joan Potter. It was rumored that Rex and his wife had seen her for marital problems over a period of two years. They didn't realize Joan was Don's sister. The implications were ugly. Hearsay suggested that Rex and his wife discovered the connection when they observed Joan sitting with Don and his wife at church. Professional oaths notwithstanding, it was highly likely that Don had heard plenty of not-so-flattering things about Rex, things that should have been held in confidence by Don's sister, but

There is No Plan

probably were not. However, we all know when it comes to juicy information, blood is truly thicker than water or any professional obligations. While intriguing, this theory had two problems. No one could confirm the story and even if it were true, no one could be sure if there was any incriminating information exchanged between patients and shrink. It could have simply been boring garden-variety marital squabbling counseling.

While some of these theories might have been true, none of them could adequately explain why Don Staton remained the VP of Sales at Rubix Adhesives. There had to be something else.

It was raining so heavily that morning at Rubix's headquarters that Rex could barely see his car in the executive parking lot as he looked out the window of his executive office. He had dreaded this day for months. He knew he needed to talk to Don and either get Rubix's sales trend turned around or let Don know he needed to plan a departure. Today was the day he was going to have that conversation with Don. Rex had planned a two-hour meeting with Don.

Don knocked on the open door of Rex's office and Rex gave the universal gesture that he should come in. Even though Rex had not specifically indicated what the subject of discussion was going to be, Don knew this was not going to be one of the standard informal business conversations they had traditionally conducted. While Don knew this was going to be a more serious meeting with Rex, he did not perceive there were any major problems with either him or his performance at Rubix. Why should he? He had not heard anything to the contrary for three years. It would have been nice for sales to grow but at least revenue levels were not slipping. Not everyone in the adhesives distribution business could claim the same. There were smaller competitors who were going backwards.

Rex's office looked like most executive offices, a standard desk with the executive's chair on one side and two visitor chairs on the other side of the desk. In addition, it also had a little table across the office with four chairs. This small table and chairs usually look like a table you would see in a breakfast area at someone's home. Rex sat down at his little table and motioned for Don to join him. They were not going to be enjoying eggs and bacon together this morning.

They started the meeting with the obligatory chitchat. Since Don perceived this was an important meeting, he was anxious to get through this required part of every meeting. While Rex and Don had a good relationship and even went to the same church, they were not particularly close nor did they spend any time outside of work together. As a result, their initial conversation was quite superficial. "How are you doing? How is your family? Can you believe this weather?" Rex was very careful not to ask any business questions because he didn't want to trivialize the important questions about Rubix's sales that he was about to pose to Don. Suddenly there was a pause in the conversation, probably only about two seconds long. This mutual hesitation indicated that the required preamble was complete and they both agreed the topic of discussion could change to the real purpose of the meeting.

"Don, you've done a great job with your entire staff and everyone seems to really like you a lot. I've heard nothing but good things about you, especially from the sales force. They really like you. I've observed on countless occasions how well you interact with your fellow executives. I enjoy working with you as well." At this point Don realized he was in more trouble than he thought. These kinds of monologues are always followed by a "but" of colossal size. The more Rex talked, the more concerned Don became. What had he done? Why was he in trouble? Was there something he had missed? Was he about to lose his job? Rex continued, "With all that being said, there is one area we need to talk about. The Board of

Comatose Management

Directors and stockholders are starting to put a lot of pressure on me to move our sales up to the next level. We've done a great job of maintaining our sales levels for the last few years, but our stockholders and directors want us to increase sales by at least five percent this coming fiscal year. Obviously, we will work on this together. I have to admit that I have not been as involved in sales as much as I should have been. I feel responsible for putting both of us in this position. I should have seen this coming. I should have had this conversation with you *before* the Board of Directors mentioned it. That is all history now. We have to look ahead and come up with a new game plan."

Don's head was spinning. He had no idea there was an ongoing concern from the Board about sales levels. However, he clearly realized that a zero percent sales growth for three years in a row would not be acceptable to the stockholders. He had been pushed off his comfortable perch for the first time at Rubix by Rex's words. He had allowed himself to think all was well. Further, he had deluded himself into thinking revenue levels at Rubix and his own personal performance were satisfactory, if not more than satisfactory. The Board of Directors and stockholders were aware of the issue and now, for the first time, Don acknowledged to himself there was a problem.

There is No Plan

How could he have lulled himself into this state? He was not angry with Rex for bringing this to his attention. He was angry with himself for blindly thinking there were no problems when in his heart of hearts he knew all along the status quo was not sustainable.

"What are your thoughts, Don?"

"I don't know where to begin, Rex. I agree with the stockholders that a lack of sales growth is undesirable. We've put in some good sales programs over the last three years, in my opinion, but we've been impeded in our growth by some of our suppliers being unable to ship products when we need them. This has undoubtedly caused us to lose a few percentage points of growth over the last two years or so."

"I agree, Don, that we've had some supply interruptions but so have all of our competitors."

Don went on, "Remember too that when I first started I inherited an inefficient and demoralized sales force. I told you when you first hired me it would take two to three years to weed out poorly performing sales management and sales representatives."

"Don, it's *been* three years since you started. More importantly, however, I'm not interested in talking about the past. It really serves no purpose at this point. I know there are many impediments

Comatose Management

to increasing sales, some of which are out of our control. Nonetheless, all of our competitors are facing the same kinds of issues and challenges we face. There is no reason for us to panic. The foundation of our sales process is good. I am not blaming you for our lack of sales growth. I should have been working with you on this from the very beginning, but I never did. I am the one who has been absentee in this area and I take responsibility. The Board of Directors and stockholders hold the CEO, me, ultimately responsible. We will get the sales growth they desire by working together and looking forward."

Don realized he was being immaturely defensive. He also was aware that Rex, as CEO, was the primary focal point for the Board when it came to any major issues at Rubix. Even though the Board looked to Rex for answers, they were going to have to fix this together or they both would ultimately suffer the consequences. Rex stood at his chair and said, "Let's take a five minute break. During that time, would you call your assistant and get her to bring two copies of your strategic sales plan to my office. We'll use this document as a starting point for a new Rubix sales plan. I'm energized by the thought of working on this with you. I love a challenge. We can do this."

There is No Plan

While there were some who thought Don Staton had a degree of executive professionalism, most agreed that Don had little in the way of substance. In short, many felt Don had a nice teacup but there was no tea. Fortunately for Don, his assistant, Wanda Kartisan, *was* quite competent and had saved him from embarrassment on more than one occasion. Wanda was as sharp as they get. Many felt if it were not for her, Don would have "resigned" about two-and-a-half years ago. She was probably smarter than Don and certainly had better people skills and knowledge of the industry. Her competence allowed Don to hide under the radar.

Rex left his office during their five-minute break. Don's head was spinning a bit again. "Strategic Sales Plan," what did Rex mean by that? Don was wondering if he had ever prepared something like that. He could not recall any documents bearing that name. He did what he always did in situations like this; he looked to Wanda for the answer. He sprinted down to Wanda's cubicle instead of calling her. He needed to talk with her in person about this and he did not want Rex walking in on their phone conversation if he called from Rex's office. "Wanda, Rex has asked for our strategic sales plan for the last two years. Do we have anything like that? We have our monthly and quarterly sales programs. Would those work? I can't think of anything else that would fit that bill?" Before Wanda could answer, he dashed into his office and googled "Strategic Sales Plan." He was desperately searching for an answer. Time was evaporating quickly. He was hoping, after he figured out what a Strategic Sales Plan *was*, that he could find a document matching the definition as closely as possible.

Just as Wanda was coming into Don's office with a pile of papers that presumably could substitute for a strategic sales plan, Don looked up and said, "I found it." He then carefully read the computer screen, "A corporate strategic sales plan represents a structured process that outlines how a company intends to sell its goods and services over a defined period. It incorporates all of the following issues in a complementary way: marketing, sales force size and skill level, sales compensation, sales management, corporate sales objectives, market segmentation, sales training, key performance indicators, objectives, goals, strategies, tactics, products and services." Don's happiness over finding this information was quickly extinguished when both Wanda and he realized there was no such plan. Wanda laid her pile of papers on Don's desk with a thud. The silence that followed

There is No Plan

was uncomfortable. What was Don to do next? Don had become the proverbial "deer caught in headlights."

Always there for Don, Wanda had an idea. She took control because Don was immobilized at that point. "I'm going to take the sales program documents for each quarter for the last two years and arrange them chronologically. I'll then bind them in two separate folders and label them 'Sales Plan.' You're going to have to buy me about fifteen minutes to get this done. Tell Rex I'll bring them to his office when I locate them." Don felt a small degree of relief. At least there was *something* he could show Rex. He thought even if it wasn't what Rex was looking for specifically, it would at least appear that some degree of sales planning was being done.

Fortunately for Don, Rex was late getting back from their break. Wanda had already delivered two professional looking folders to Rex's office before he returned. Each had "Sales Plan - Fiscal Year" labels on them. They were also rather voluminous in size. Don actually allowed himself to relax a little and even recover some confidence. Rex looked at the folders and said, "Thanks for getting these for us." Don watched as Rex opened up the first one and quickly leafed through it. He then opened up the second one and skimmed

Comatose Management

through it at an even faster rate. "Don, these are nothing more than your quarterly sales programs. These are just your short-term sales incentive programs. I must have confused you. I'm looking for your Rubix Annual Strategic Sales Plan. Can you call Wanda and get her to bring it down?" There was a long silence.

Don knew not to take this game any further. He looked at Rex and said, "We don't have a plan like you are looking for. This is the closest we come to a plan like that."

Now it was time for Rex's head to do some spinning. In this moment, he realized Rubix had not been operating under any kind of sales plan for three years, maybe even longer. No wonder they had problems growing the revenue. There was no sales rudder on this ship. He was simultaneously mad at Don and at himself. How could this have gone on so long? Why had Don never taken the initiative to do this? Why had Rex not seen this obvious gap? Did Don even know *how* to do this? Rex did not know what else to do other than to look at Don and say, "That's all right. We'll come up with one together."

Don was very apologetic to Rex. Rex simply repeated to Don, "That's all right. We'll come up with a plan together. We're looking forward."

"Thank you for understanding, Rex; this is my shortcoming. I have an idea that could get us up to speed. I know it's probably not particularly detailed, but why don't we take your last two Board of Directors' reports and pull out the sales projections and strategies information. It will give us something to work from and it will ensure that we are providing the Board a consistent message when we roll out a new plan." Rex was getting mildly irritated that suddenly Don was using the word "we" much more than before. Suddenly it was a "we" problem. Was Don not the VP of Sales? Was this not his area of responsibility? Rex felt Don was upwardly delegating the sales planning responsibility. Nevertheless, he remembered that as CEO he was ultimately responsible and had said as much to Don.

"Do you have a copy of those plans in your office?" asked Don. Rex now felt he had to reestablish the hierarchy.

"Don, I don't know how much of my reporting to the Board can help us here. Let's reconvene tomorrow morning in my office at 8:00 a.m. Before we meet tomorrow, I want to warn you that much of my reporting to the Board is considered privileged information. Why don't you see if you and Wanda can find anything else that could help."

Comatose Management

Rex knew he had never presented any kind of specific sales strategies to the Board. CEOs run corporations; they do not plan specific sales activities. Or do they? Besides, the Board had never asked for any kind of strategic sales plan. All they had ever asked for was end of quarter revenues and projected next quarter revenues. That was it. Should he have been providing more detailed sales planning and strategies information? As an expert in sales, one would think Don Staton, VP of Sales, would have simply provided this to Rex and he could have distilled it down for the Board. Don had let him down. All Rex could find in his office were old end of quarter revenue numbers and revenue projections. That was it. There was nothing.

When Rex walked into his office the next morning at 7:30 a.m. he found Don already sitting at the little table with some documents in front of him. There was even a possible hint of a smirk on Don's face. Rex was a little angry that Don had invaded his space. Who did he think he was, coming into the CEO's office before the appointed time? The first thing out of Don's mouth was, "Were you able to find anything?"

Rex felt Don knew the answer to that question already. However, Rex realized that possibly all of this stress was making him paranoid. Don was

There is No Plan

probably just asking a simple question and was trying to help. Rex looked him straight in the eye and answered, "I did, but it is privileged information and can only be viewed by the CEO and the Board of Directors." Don knew Rex was lying, but it was understandable. Rex, as CEO, did not want to look as incompetent to Don as Don was looking to Rex. He thought, how stupid does Rex think I am? Rex could tell by Don's expression that he knew he was lying. Rex could not leave it alone, however. He added, "I'll do the best I can to use some of the information. I'll need to be careful to only reveal information the Board will not recognize as coming from this privileged information." There is nothing worse than a liar who adds details after he has been busted. Rex concluded this topic by saying, "We'll have to start from scratch essentially, which is not necessarily a bad thing."

At that moment in time, they both comprehended the unthinkable for a $1.1 billion corporation. There was no sales plan. They both thought the other person had one. Neither the CEO, the Board of Directors or the VP of Sales had in their possession anything resembling a sales plan for Rubix Adhesives, Inc. Additionally, no one asked for one until Rex did yesterday, and the only reason he asked for one was that the Board and shareholders were putting the pressure on.

Comatose Management

The stockholders would not have been pleased to learn this.

Rex and Don met two days later specifically to put together a strategic sales plan that would be palatable to the Board of Directors and the stockholders. Rex was able to find some examples of plans from other companies where he sat on their Boards. Don went to the public library and did not find anything. In the end, Don ended up printing about 200 pages worth of examples he found by googling "strategic sales plan." They sat for all of two hours in Rex's office, at the ubiquitous kitchen table found in every executive's office, and assembled a plan.

Wanda, Don's enabling assistant, took what they had done and reformulated it into a document that actually had a stream of consciousness and looked well thought out. Don was quite proud of himself for having the last-minute idea to get a fancy binder made by the marketing department, something that would give it more sizzle to the Board, in his opinion. Sadly, this was probably his biggest contribution to the entire process. The document, in its ornate binder, was sent to the Board of Directors and to the Regional VPs of Sales in all of the countries where they operated. Within six months, sales had increased one-and-a-half percent over the same period in the prior fiscal year. This was not a stellar improvement but a significant step up over the prior five years. Over the next six month period sales increased two-and-a-quarter percent over the same period in the prior fiscal year. While hardly a scientific study, this at least anecdotally indicated to Rex and Don that *any* plan is better than *no* plan.

Full year over year sales had increased three-and-three-quarters percent. The Board was ecstatic. One would hope the Board's enthusiasm said more about their low expectations of their senior leadership than it did about the Board's naiveté. While Rubix was behind their competitors' average growth by eight-and-one-quarter percent, it was a "victory" nonetheless, if only a relative one. Rex's self-appointed Board cited "continued growth" as the justification for giving Rex Bolden, CEO of Rubix Adhesives, Inc., a $750,000 performance bonus for the year. Don Staton, VP of Sales for Rubix Adhesives, Inc. was promoted to Executive VP of Sales with a $100,000 increase in his base salary. Champagne corks were flying everywhere.

"That doesn't seem fair to the shareholders on so many levels," Zack suddenly injected.

"Zack, most of the shareholders don't *want* to know what's going on. It's much easier to pretend everyone is competent and doing a good job with their investment."

2
EMPOWERED IMPOSTERS

⌘ ⌘ ⌘

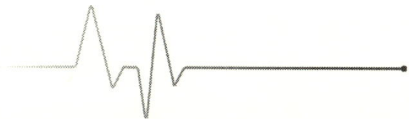

I love Starbucks. It is a great place for conversation. Zack and I had both just settled down at a comfortable table with our venti coffees when I saw a Lamborghini sports car pull up. Very expensive. Very Italian. A sixtyish man got out of the driver's seat, ran around the back of the car and opened the passenger door for his "this-could-be-my-daughter" girlfriend. Zack and I both looked at each other with a knowing grin. This image made me recall a dysfunctional behavior I frequently observe in management. It may seem unlikely that a middle-aged man, a sports car and a young girlfriend could teach us about a management dysfunction, but they can. This unspoken dysfunctional behavior is found in many

Comatose Management

organizations. Once identified and isolated, it addresses and answers many inconsistencies found in those organizations. My experiences during my career have helped me understand more fully why so many companies exhibit this maladaptive practice, especially at the top. For example, how can large publicly owned corporations pay astronomical salaries and bonuses to their CEO's when company stock values are in the basement? The craziest part is that it appears very few people notice the incongruities caused by this dysfunction. Those who are blind to this practice appear to be operating at some level of denial.

    I had my initial indoctrination regarding this phenomenon while I was working for a Fortune 500 company. At first I didn't say anything to anyone, but as time went on, I mentioned it to a few select confidants and most agreed that it existed and that it was hurting the business. After leaving that company, I noticed this same dysfunction in many other companies I dealt with.

    "If you've got the time this morning, Zack, I'd like to tell you a story about how corporations sometimes believe things are working one way when they are really working just the opposite. Like that older guy who just parked his Lamborghini. He may actually believe that his arm-candy makes him appear young, cool and handsome. He has come to believe it over time because, out of social courtesy, no one ever says otherwise."

Zack sat back in his chair, ready to listen, and I began.

Marcus had worked at Abrasives and Cutting Tools, Inc. for about six months when a situation arose that created a need for him to urgently talk with the President of the Company. Marcus had been hired as a sales manager and had been assigned a sales force of 20 salespeople. The total number of employees for the Company was about 150. Marcus suspected one of his people was an alcoholic and had come to work drunk. Sarah was not somewhat tipsy. She was drunk, slurring her words and literally stumbling down the aisle on the way to her cubicle. Marcus reported to the VP of Sales, but he was out that day and Marcus thought this was urgent enough that he should talk to the President, David Patten. He had considered going to Human Resources to get an answer, but their role was limited to what it is in most companies, finding candidates to hire and handling the payroll and benefits. No, he decided to talk directly to David Patten about Sarah. However, he had mixed feelings about bringing this directly to David's attention.

Comatose Management

The Company President was known for many things, but two that stood out the most to Marcus were his office and his income. Both were intimidating. He obviously projected wealth because he had a model of a jet on a big mahogany desk. Not only did he have the model, but he also had the *real* thing. The carpet in his office was at least three-quarters of an inch thick. It reminded Marcus of the carpeting he used to see in the 1970's, but David's was brand new. Adjoining David's office was a conference room that was only reserved for the Executive Board. It had a nameplate on the outside that read President's Executive Conference Room. It seemed somewhat funny to Marcus that a company with 150 employees would need a conference room like this, much less have *eight* executives to fill the seats. That would be like IBM having something like 7,000 souls on their Board of Directors. Seemed like a little overkill.

Bitsie was the President's assitant and despite the fact that there were only 150 employees at Abrasives and Cutting Tools, Inc., you had to be escorted into David's office by Bitsie no matter who you were. It was quite a formal affair. One could almost compare the seriousness of this entrance with that of meeting the U. S. Secretary of State. That is how David certainly imagined it. David

Empowered Imposters

was very proud to tell everyone he had started Abrasives and Cutting Tools, Inc. some 30 years ago. He thought he was very shrewd by naming the Company as he did because it not only told everyone what business they were in but it also created an acronym of ACT. He was constantly saying, "We are in the abrasives and cutting tools business, and to be successful we must all *act* together and take *act*ion." There was only one problem with his story. He did not start the Company; his dad did. Amazingly, only a handful of employees were aware of this because he did such a phenomenal job of covering up this little inconvenient fact. Marcus was aware that David's dad had started the Company but it did not matter to him at all. David had been running it for more than 30 years. He had proven himself.

After being properly presented to David by Bitsie, Marcus began to tell him the situation. David was extremely agitated as Marcus told him the details of how Sarah had come to work intoxicated and was hardly able to sit in her chair at that very moment. Marcus went on to provide additional details about his suspicions regarding her drinking problems and how everything seemed to lead up to this moment. David finally got out of his executive chair and stood behind it, grasping it firmly from behind. He appeared to be doing some kind of exercises behind his chair while holding on to it firmly. All of this was going on while David was talking. Marcus was very concerned about David's behavior. Was David signaling to Marcus that he was unhappy that he brought this matter into his presence? Had Marcus overstepped his boundaries? Had he committed a major faux pas by bringing this to the company President? Was David feeling okay?

While still gyrating behind his executive chair, David looked at Marcus and said, "There is no problem here. We've known for a long time that Sarah has a drinking problem from time to time, but she has always seemed to manage her way around it. Why don't you just send her home for the day and call it a sick day?" This did not seem right to Marcus, but he respected David so much that he quickly concluded this was the proper course of action given all the variables. Marcus immediately left David's office, talked with Sarah and she went home by 8:30 a.m. Marcus had a feeling in his gut when he was talking with Sarah that she had been through this precise ritual many times before at ACT. For the first time since he had started working for David, he wondered if David handled things in the right way. He did not feel good about it.

Empowered Imposters

Now that the "Sarah problem" was taken care of (at least for the day), Marcus could get back to work. He had gotten his desk organized for the day and poured himself a cup of bad corporate coffee, fresh from the nasty looking drip coffee machine in the breakroom. As he was going through his emails he looked up for a second and saw something that was increasingly becoming an annoyance to Marcus. Normally this did not really bother him that much, but after the Sarah thing in the morning this really got on his nerves. David Patten was standing by Julie Nelson's cubicle. Julie was an account manager and the prettiest girl in the office, by far. She also worked for Marcus. Not only was David standing there, but he was holding on to the walls of her cubicle and doing that little dance of his, moving his hips back and forth and sideways, just like he did behind his executive chair in his office earlier that morning. The dance was beginning to get on Marcus's nerves, but his hourly flirting with Julie was becoming even more of a problem. Julie had no choice but to sit there and listen to him while watching his little aerobic routine. David interpreted her willingness to listen as her being interested in him. Everyone knew that Julie was *not* interested.

David was one of those people who had reached his late fifties but felt entitled to still act

Comatose Management

like a man in his thirties. His level of entitlement was expressed in the age inappropriate clothes he wore and the cars he drove - he should have had a license tag on them that read MACC, Middle Age Crisis Car. David was about 60 pounds overweight and it showed too. He also managed to have a handful of very young girlfriends who apparently had repeatedly kept him up past his bedtime because he looked every one of his 57 years and then some.

Shortly after the Sarah episode, Julie began to question why she had stayed so many years at ACT. The work atmosphere was not very positive and the facilities were rundown and depressing, except for David's office, of course. She had been feeling bad about her job and started feeling physically sick as well. She thought it was a result of her job, but was shocked to find out that it was something much more serious. After many medical tests, she received a colon cancer diagnosis. She was admitted for treatment to Barnett Hospital. After going through several surgeries and chemotherapy to treat her cancer Julie ultimately reached the end of her rope with David when he called her in her hospital room after one of her surgeries. With Julie's left arm plugged into a morphine drip and her right holding up the phone David asked her, "What was the name of that cute girl you introduced me to at that seminar a couple of months ago? I'd like to call her." Julie was a little upset, even on morphine, that David asked her a question like that in her current condition. He did not even bother with any obligatory formalities such as, "How are you doing?" After that moment Julie didn't have any more time for David and decided to no longer oblige his immature and inappropriate flirting with her at the office. He was creepy in her opinion and she was going to stop pretending that he was not.

Marcus was able to ignore much of David's unusual behavior, such as his rock-and-roll antics while holding on to solid objects. Most of the managers made fun of David's idiosyncratic behaviors that included the inability to converse. That's right. David was unable to carry on a conversation beyond one to two sentences. It was commonly believed the reason for this was that David was extremely brilliant and unable to really engage those of average intelligence. Another oddity with David was his work hours. He worked about 15 to 20 hours per week. Marcus and the rest of the management employees figured that brilliant and creative types march to the beat of their own drum. The majority had nothing but respect for him, despite some dents on the fender.

Comatose Management

Despite David's dysfunctional behavior, Julie's struggle with cancer and Marcus's growing disillusionment, there were some good things happening at ACT, at least from a sales perspective. Julie was working almost full-time again after her latest release from the hospital. She was working on several big deals. Abrasives and Cutting Tools, Inc. was on the verge of getting one of the biggest orders it had ever received. Marcus was especially pleased about the pending order because he had been instrumental in taking it all the way to third base. Julie and he had worked hard to secure this order. Both Julie and Marcus thought that after a one-hour meeting with the customer at the ACT home office they would get a signed contract. The company that was about to purchase this large amount of product was a prospect that had never done business with ACT before, even further sweetening the deal in Marcus's eyes. Big order. New Customer. Recognition. It does not get any better than that in sales. The customer insisted on having a final meeting at ACT headquarters. This was not unusual for a first time customer at ACT. They wanted to see what ACT's home looked like before marrying the daughter. Marcus got even more excited about the deal when he realized David Patten was going to attend this meeting. Having the President attend an important

Empowered Imposters

customer meeting like this adds a tremendous amount of credibility.

The meeting was scheduled for the next day in the main conference room and Marcus was excited. It was an acceptable conference room, but nothing fancy. The chairs were a little worn and the carpeting probably should have been replaced about three years ago. The long wooden table had a handful of water glass stains on it but nothing that some company collateral could not cover - literally. There was a nameplate on the outside of this room that read, Patten Conference Room. Marcus asked Julie if it might be smarter to have the customer meeting in the President's Executive Conference Room. She immediately responded, "David only allows *executives* in his conference room. He would never let us use it for customers." Then Marcus thought, but it is these customers that pay for the conference rooms and his outlandish salary and perks. "Marcus, I've been through this with David about twenty times; we won't be able to use the nicer conference room." David consistently chose to rigorously enforce his mandate regarding the "executives only in the Executive Conference Room" policy and it probably hurt sales and the company as a whole. However, Marcus thought, David must have a good reason for this policy. Julie and I just aren't experienced enough to understand it. David is President for a reason.

The customer meeting started out well. Four representatives from the prospective customer showed up for the meeting, which is always a good sign. The more people a potential customer commits, the more interested they are. More skin in the game, literally. Marcus and Julie had carefully cleaned up the Patten Conference Room and had coffee and donuts available too. The first ten minutes of the meeting consisted of nothing more than the usual hand shaking and business card swapping. There was only one problem at this point. Marcus had made a big deal about how the company President was going to attend, but he had not shown. The introduction part of the meeting was quickly ending and Marcus did not know what he should do. He quietly dispatched Julie to see if she could find him. As she walked out of the room she whispered to Marcus, "Don't set your expectations too high." Marcus was not exactly sure what she meant by that, but he was soon going to find out.

Julie quickly returned to the conference room and told Marcus that David was just pulling his car into his executive parking space. He was driving his Corvette today. Marcus started to become visibly upset when Julie said to him, "This is

Empowered Imposters

normal for David; he'll get here when he gets here. We need to start the meeting and make some kind of excuse for David. I've got a whole bag full of them from past experience." Marcus told the customer attendees that David had an "executive emergency" and would be delayed momentarily. He did not feel great about that explanation, but it was the best he could come up with considering his anger and disappointment. Julie started the PowerPoint presentation without David's presence and was doing a good job considering the potential for sheer boredom that many PowerPoint presentations can inflict. Twenty minutes into the presentation, in walked David Patten, President of Abrasives and Cutting Tools, Inc. He did not slip in; he made a grand entrance. The presentation came to a complete stop while everyone was introduced to David Patten, President of Abrasives and Cutting Tools, Inc.

   David completely took over the meeting at that point. Both Julie and Marcus could see a level of confusion and concern in their customers' faces. They had a look of, "Who is this guy. Who does he think he is, blowing in here like this? It is disrespectful to everyone to behave in this manner." Marcus quickly realized that this was not Julie's first rodeo with David. Her facial expressions were completely neutral as the meeting

Comatose Management

went from productive to insane. She had obviously seen this before. Why had she not warned Marcus? He thought maybe this was a crazy selling strategy he had never seen before and maybe everything was okay. David was the President and he was brilliant after all. Marcus felt maybe he should just relax.

The customer contingent that had arrived that day was considering buying a substantial initial inventory of product for all 300 of their North American branches. It would be a multi-million dollar order. Marcus quickly realized that, because of David's antics, the deal was in danger of being lost. The rest of the meeting was an equal mixture of comedy and horror to Marcus. The customer asked David how long it would take ACT to supply all 300 of their branches and David answered by talking about ACT's new office facility. The customer asked David if ACT could accommodate an automatic replenishment program at their branches and he answered by discussing, at length, the new shelving and material handling equipment they had in their warehouse. The questions went on and on like this. Marcus began to figure out that the customer's meeting participants were getting a kick out of David's nuttiness and were just egging him on at this point. Marcus had been in sales for many years. He knew the deal was lost. David had established that the top leadership of the Company appeared to be incompetent – or worse. For the first time, Marcus began to see cracks in David's foundation. At the end of the meeting (which went on for almost three hours because David could not stop talking), the customer attendees performed the necessary handshakes and obligatory parting statements. Marcus knew that the deal was dead and David had killed it. "The deal is dead, but long live the king," he thought. As David walked out of the room you could tell he was extremely proud of his performance by his body language. Head held high, shoulders back and a proud walk. He was the king after all.

Marcus motioned to Julie to come to his office as soon as possible. When she entered his office she still had a neutral expression on her face. Had she not been at the meeting? Did she not see what had happened? Her first words to Marcus were, "You obviously did not ensure that David wasn't going to be at the meeting."

"What do you mean?" he said.

"Some of us know that David will kill any deal he gets near. We always make sure to plan customer meetings at the office when we know David is going to be out of the office or we can create some other diversion."

Comatose Management

Marcus asked, "Why didn't someone tell me about this? I have never heard any of this before."

"I just assumed you knew this, Marcus, but I guess I was wrong. My assumption has cost me a lot of commission. I've been here long enough to know David is like that. No one really talks about it."

Marcus asked, "What other things do I need to know about David?"

Julie began to fill Marcus in on the things he wished he had known before even accepting the job. It was one of the worst days of his life. "David is an alcoholic. I can't believe that you and so many other people don't see that. Why do you think he was so easy on Sarah the other day when she came in drunk? Yes, everyone knows about her coming in drunk. David is an alcoholic and can empathize with her. He also abuses drugs, mainly marijuana and cocaine. Why do you think he can't ever sit still? Why do you think he constantly has to physically hold on to things? He's trying to keep his balance. He is high on cocaine. I estimate that he is high about one-third of the time he is in the office. Unfortunately, he has even offered drugs to some of my customers he mistakenly thought might be interested. Talk about the need for damage control. David is not up to the job of being the President but everyone pretends he is.

Empowered Imposters

Why do you think he pretends to own a jet when he doesn't? He is just a one-fourth renter of it, by the way. He wants to look important. Why do you think he insists on so much grandiosity surrounding his office? He wants to at least look like a king. He knows he is a management imposter."

Marcus asked Julie, "How has he been able to get away with this all these years?"

Julie continued with her blunt honesty. "Because he has been fortunate enough to have some good employees who prop him up and his dad started a business that in most ways runs itself. Warren Buffet's philosophy is that one should only buy businesses an idiot can run, because eventually they will be run by an idiot. This is one of those businesses. You probably don't know he didn't start the business either, I suppose." Marcus replied that he did in fact know that detail about David but had chosen not to let it negatively color his feelings about David even though David lied about it all the time.

Julie went on, "When I first started here I noticed that David didn't seem like much of a manager, much less a company President. I'm too blunt for my own good; I couldn't help asking people what the situation with David was. The most comical answer I got was from Bitsie, his

Comatose Management

'executive assistant.' She said, 'Julie, the only way I can answer you is to tell you that still waters run deep.' She told me that David appears a little dim-witted on the surface but is genius deep within. Just like deep waters, the surface may be still but down below there is a torrent of activity. I wasn't buying it, but it seemed like most of the others were. I was beginning to realize at that point David was an imposter manager and the employees were enabling it to happen. The employees at ACT have quite literally empowered him to be a fake. He is an Empowered Imposter. I think he knows he is incompetent which is why he surrounds himself with all the trappings of royalty. The people who aren't willing to wake up and realize what is going on are allowing this to go on year after year. Most of us can't stand the idea of the President being a knucklehead so we unconsciously make him a hero and explain away all of his idiosyncrasies. We actively resist processing the information right under our noses. The individual employees give him the power to continue his ruse. I say *individual* because out of 150 ACT employees there are a few who have figured out what I'm saying. It's happening one person at a time and the numbers are growing. There will be a tipping point. At some time in the future there will be some kind of mass exodus, overthrow or mutiny."

"Marcus, have you ever thought about the salary that David gets? He makes three times our salary and gets a hefty bonus two times a year, not to mention all the benefits he lavishes on himself. ACT's bankers and seven other executives should know that David doesn't represent top management potential in corporate America. How do they rationalize his incompetency while he is simultaneously compensated beyond any reasonable level, especially based on his lack of management abilities? It's called cognitive dissonance, Marcus. Cognitive dissonance simply means that when we observe something inconsistent with what we know, we will create in our mind a *reality* that makes things rational again. I see that David is incompetent and is compensated irrationally. The bankers and ACT executives see David as a brilliant entrepreneur with idiosyncrasies. It all makes sense that way to them. They think David is a paragon of the industry and because he is so gifted, he is expected to have a multitude of odd habits; everyone knows that geniuses are eccentric. These behaviors are killing ACT unfortunately. David's "contributions" shouldn't be compensated, they need to be eliminated."

Julie continued, "David sending Sarah home when she was drunk with no consequence wasn't

Comatose Management

kindness; it was poor judgment. David's flagrant flirtation with me isn't charming or endearing; it's creepy and illegal. David's alcohol and drug abuse aren't character flaws associated with genius; they're reckless and illegal activity. David's need for executive decorum doesn't represent his ability; it represents his need to *look* like he has abilities. David's complete inability to make coherent statements with customers isn't a character trait; it's killing our ability to attract new business. All of the things ACT employees do to empower David as an imposter hurt the business. We, the company employees, are responsible for enabling David to be an Empowered Imposter. Don't you understand?"

Marcus sat there listening to Julie talk about these issues and suddenly he felt very stupid. He felt stupid for not realizing these things himself. They were so obvious but he chose not to see them. He thought back to when he first started at ACT. He realized that he did have some concerns about David's aberrant behavior but never allowed himself to process the thoughts. He did not want to think the company was being managed by an imposter, an Empowered Imposter. Marcus was, to some extent, responsible for the Company being managed by David and for all the damage David caused. Some of that damage he had just witnessed when they lost a good potential customer because of David's silly antics.

When Marcus first started with ACT he remembered consciously thinking, either David Patten is the most brilliant CEO in the world or a complete idiot. He had chosen the former, and was wrong. He did not want to face the reality that not everyone in a management position is competent just because he or she has the title and the trappings. Marcus also realized that at this moment there were others besides David in the organization who were Empowered Imposters. He asked Julie straightforwardly, "Are there other people like David in the organization? I mean, are there other Empowered Imposters?"

Julie answered with an astute answer, "Of course there are. Moreover, the people who work for them empower them just as David has been empowered. Remember Marcus, exactly fifty percent of all physicians graduated in the bottom half of their class. Just because you have the title does not mean you know what you are doing. Legitimate and capable managers know this fact and are constantly looking for and preventing Empowered Imposters and removing them or providing remediation."

When we empower imposters it makes us stupid, Marcus thought. We all suffer by

Comatose Management

denying reality and empowering - maybe even *encouraging* - management that is hurting the Company. Individual employees suffer, as does the business as a whole. Everyone has to work under poor leadership while doing the biddings of the Empowered Imposter.

As Marcus walked out to his car to drive home that night, he was reminded of a TV show he saw as a child. It was a Three Stooges episode created before he was even born, but represented everything Julie had taught him that day. The Stooges all dressed up as physicians in a legitimate hospital. Clearly, the Stooges had no idea what they were doing, but they looked the part, had the right title (Dr.) and were in the right place to be physicians. The other doctors at the hospital, who actually had medical degrees, could not understand the bizarre and random techniques these three visiting physicians were using on patients. In order for the world to make sense to the staff doctors, they decided these visiting doctors were brilliant and their techniques were beyond their understanding. Instead of questioning them, the hospital staff doctors were worshipping them. The legitimate physicians had completely empowered the imposters. In reality, the Three Stooges were complete idiots who knew absolutely nothing about medicine.

Empowered Imposters

The fact that Julie brought all of this to Marcus's attention made him question whether *he* was an Empowered Imposter himself.

"Zack, I hope this story helps you make better decisions about how you interact with your employer and fellow employees. Our minds can play tricks on us in order to make all the pieces fit."

3
THE PRODUCTIVE EMPLOYEE

⌘ ⌘ ⌘

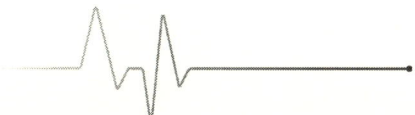

We were standing in line at our regular Starbucks when Zack looked at me and said, "Look at that barista. She's working with her hands and actually producing something. Technology has created a world in which people don't really have to work anymore. We just sit in front of our computers all day. It's hard to believe the world can continue like that. Somebody has to do real work like that barista making coffee behind the counter. It seems like white collar workers don't make a significant contribution to the economy anymore because they just stare into their computer screens all day."

"I understand what you are saying, Zack, but it's not as simple as that. First, only a small percentage of the population has jobs that require them to sit in front of a computer all day. Would you believe only 20 years ago it was considered a sign of lowered status for an executive to have a computer on his or her desk? Important people didn't have computers or monitors at their desks. People who did *important* work had no need for computers. I even remember a junior VP of Marketing named Eric at a Fortune 500 company who had his assistant *print* his emails. His ego and lack of understanding of technology caused him to misuse the technology available to him. That has changed 100 percent. If you don't have a computer on your desk these days, many people might think you must have a menial job. Interestingly, Barack Obama is the first President of the U.S. to put a computer on the desk in the Oval Office. This one action represents a much needed change in Presidential thinking."

"Two Grandes with room," yelled the barista.

"So you're saying that technology is associated with status?" asked Zack between sips of coffee.

"Yes. I think most people would agree that jobs associated with technology are considered higher level and generally pay better than blue collar careers."

Zack seemed a little frustrated. "I'm saying that sitting in front of a computer is not real

The Productive Employee

work, but you're saying that sitting in front of one implies status. According to what you just said, the status thing has only happened in the last 20 years. Can we agree then that jobs that rely heavily on technology have status but don't really accomplish any actual work? At the same time, are we also in harmony if I say jobs that don't rely on technology – blue collar jobs – are the engine of the world economy but appear near the bottom of the career caste system?"

"Whoa! Zack you are making this both too complicated and overly simplistic at the same time. The blue-collar versus white-collar value issue has been around since the industrial revolution. This is essentially what we are talking about. Is sitting behind a desk typing on a computer more valuable than man and machine welding iron on an assembly line? Is the pilot sitting behind the controls of a jet more valuable than the person fueling the plane, allowing it to fly in the first place? Rightly or wrongly, our world seems to value the technology worker more highly. This is evidenced by the higher compensation these roles normally receive."

"But it doesn't seem fair that someone should be valued more highly and compensated more richly for just pushing buttons when others are doing the real work," added Zack.

Comatose Management

"And that is precisely where you are oversimplifying things, Zack. If you think of technology as a tool, I think it will clear things up for you a bit. In the 19th century, the skilled blacksmith, using the tools of his trade, made more money than the person who picked potatoes for a living. The blacksmith had to know how to use his tools and had to be intelligent enough to use them in a way that created value for his customers."

"Okay I get it," chimed in Zack. "If you use tools you get paid more because you have to know how to use them. That makes sense to me. What do you mean by 'intelligent enough' to use them?"

"And that, Zack, is the crux of things. It wasn't the tools themselves that allowed the blacksmith to make more money than the individual who picked potatoes; it was his ability to use them. The more intelligent the blacksmith, the more he could leverage his knowledge and skills. An intelligent blacksmith with a high level of knowledge *and* the right tools would have been extremely productive and valued. His tools were a way for him to realize and put into form what he knew. It allowed him to literally capture and sculpt what his mind could conceive. The individual potato picker could have owned the blacksmith's tools, but they would have

The Productive Employee

been of no value to him if he didn't know how to use them. 'Technology' is just an umbrella term we currently use to describe some of the tools available to us today."

"Will there be a time when technology tools will not require human intervention?" wondered Zack.

"Yes. There are those who argue that we've already reached that point if you consider robotic assembly plants for example. However, if we reverse engineer robots, we realize they are run by computers guided by complex software programs written and maintained by people. When we are able to simulate human thought processes very accurately – this is called artificial intelligence – we might then be able to say we have divorced man from machine. When human intervention at the hardware and software level is no longer necessary, we might be at that point. That, my friend, is many years away and the progress toward that goal has been slow. Very slow."

"Zack, the questions you are asking have a profound impact on business. Many companies don't know how to separate the following: motivation, tools, skills and intelligence. They tend to blend them all together and view them as one. It can make managing a business difficult and inefficient. I've observed several areas where companies commonly get these confused. Let me give you some examples.

"I was working with a small to medium sized distributor of industrial fasteners a few years ago whose warehouse operations had frankly turned into a disaster area. Not only were they falling behind in their work, but they were also being plagued by the following problems:

- o Shipping errors galore
- o Huge amounts of returned merchandise
- o A growing pile of special products not connected to any customers
- o A growing number of backorders
- o A mounting number of incoming shipments sitting on the dock
- o Extremely unhappy salespeople
- o Most importantly, dissatisfied customers

Worst of all they had little or no idea where they stood on these problems. Were things getting worse or were they getting better?"

"Sounds like things were pretty bad, at least in their warehouse," added Zack.

"They were. There were many meetings regarding how to fix all of these warehouse problems. It was funny that the meetings themselves came to be viewed as the fix, as if

The Productive Employee

just having the meetings was the prescription for the illness. 'Everything is going to be okay; we're having meetings to fix the problems.' The salespeople in particular were not impressed. They were the front-line soldiers actually having to deal with these weaknesses.

"After many of these meetings, it was decided that everyone in the warehouse just needed to work harder. The President of the company even weighed in on things and noted that not only did the hourly warehouse workers need to work harder, but warehouse management needed to work harder too. As an outsider listening in, you cannot imagine how empty these comments sounded. I wanted to ask the company President where he thought transportation would be today if, starting 2,000 years ago, the human race did nothing more than encourage horses to run faster in order to expedite the delivery of goods to market. This was an example of a company focusing on tasks without questioning the tools they were using. They also failed to ask whether the warehouse workers and warehouse management had the necessary skills. Finally, were they hiring the right kinds of people? We've all heard the expression that you can't turn a plow horse into a racehorse. The 'work harder' strategy did nothing but encourage the employees to find other employment and the company is now just a shadow of what it was in its prime."

"It seems most people would understand there is more to fixing problems than just working harder," Zack added.

"You are right about that."

Zack went on, "Even small businesses are more complex than that. If, and that is a big 'if,' one could get workers to work harder, doesn't it seem obvious that many of their root problems would simply be amplified further? If we amplify a bad radio signal it only makes the static louder."

"You have impressed me, Zack. You are exactly right. Now I'd like to tell you about a company that is the complete opposite of the one we just discussed. This company had a fantastic work ethic. Everyone in the company seemed to work hard all of the time. It was actually quite amazing to observe. Even more surprising was that these hard working employees worked hard because they seemed to love their jobs and the company. I initially wondered why they brought me in to take a look at things. On the surface, all seemed well. I was soon to learn otherwise.

"After looking under the covers, I came to the realization they had many problems. They appeared to be on the entrance ramp of the long road to bankruptcy.

The Productive Employee

"They had about 200 employees, manufactured custom telecom equipment subassemblies, and sold them to large manufacturers for inclusion in their hardware. It was 1999, the height of the telecom boom. One would expect everything to be as wonderful as an outdoor barbecue with Robin Williams. However, things weren't so good.

"Their manufacturing and warehousing processes and systems seemed to be working well. Manufacturing was able to keep up with anything in the pipeline. After careful research, I realized their order pipeline was the problem. They didn't know what was in it. They had a nice steady stream of orders, but these orders weren't being transmitted to manufacturing or to their warehouse. They literally had the products in their warehouse or could readily manufacture them but no one seemed to know exactly what was being ordered. It was as if they were a fueled airplane sitting on the runway ready for takeoff and no one from the control tower was telling them to go."

"So, what were the issues causing this?"

"Very good question, Zack. Most issues like this have multiple root problems, but in this case, it was really just one. Fear of technology."

"Fear of technology, what does that mean?"

Comatose Management

"While their manufacturing and warehousing capabilities were rather impressive, their information technology infrastructure was a three-car-pileup. Back in the 1980's they had installed their first computer system. They had wisely purchased a business tool that kept them competitive. By today's standards, however, it was a miniscule computer with virtually no capabilities. It was initially purchased to simply accept an order and transmit basic information to manufacturing and to their warehouse. Everything worked well for many years until their order volume started to overwhelm the limited capabilities of their 1980's computer system.

"Instead of upgrading their computer equipment, they tried to push more out of their existing system and save money. This was not a good decision for a number of reasons. First, performance versus cost on new systems was dramatically better than equipment from the 1980's. Second, they were going to unnecessarily spend an enormous amount of money on programmers and systems specialists in order to keep their Model T on the highway. To make things worse (and more expensive), there was a dwindling number of people who knew how to work on their antiquated system. Finally, there was no new software being developed for their old system. Not only had there been significant advances in hardware, but manufacturing software had made great strides too. Unfortunately, this new and better software wasn't able to run on their current hardware.

"This company had failed to realize that working hard with old tools was causing them to fall behind their competitors. Where would we be today if we still used the telegraph as our primary means of 'high speed' communication? Just as we need to work hard, improve our skills and hire intelligent people, we also need to upgrade and update our tools in order to be competitive. Tools can quickly reach a point of diminishing returns when their contributions to productivity are eclipsed by better tools being used by our competitors."

"The fact they had a computer at all would have helped their efficiency, correct?"

"You are right, Zack. However, that would only be true if they operated in a vacuum. Their competitors had moved on to computers that were able to provide more information in a shorter timeframe and in a more cost effective way. This company was figuratively still using wood-handled hammers to break rocks when their competitors had moved on to pneumatic jackhammers. The competitive outcome of upgrading to better tools is usually quite predictable and measurable."

"You've talked about people working harder and using up to date tools. There is an ingredient here you haven't mentioned yet. Skills. If we find the hardest working people and provide the best tools, but they don't know what they're doing, aren't we headed for disaster?"

"Precisely, Zack. A great example of this, and one that I see almost every day, is in sales. A really motivated sales professional with all the latest tools available will usually do quite poorly if he or she doesn't have the essential skills needed."

"What tools and skills are you talking about?" Zack asked.

"The tools could include CRM (Customer Relationship Management), PDA's (Personal Digital Assistant) and smartphones. CRM is a software tool that allows an organization to track the details of customer activity, identify prospects, forecast sales, etc. PDA's and smartphones provide not only phone capability, but are basically personal computers you can hold in your hand. CRM access is available on these PDA's and smartphones. These are just some of the tools available to sales organizations. And just like all other business tools, these tools continue to evolve as well. Tools are great, but without the knowledge and skills to properly use them and integrate them into the business, they can become a hindrance.

"One of the many skills necessary for sales professionals to be successful is a hands-on knowledge of the products and services their organization offers. It would be hard to imagine how a sales professional could succeed without knowing how the customer uses what he or she is selling.

"Sales skills, specific to his or her industry, are also needed. I'm not talking about the sales techniques taught in the 1950's. I'm talking about current sales concepts. Customers and prospects are much more sophisticated than they were even ten years ago. They can see a canned sales technique coming at them from 20 miles away. And it turns them off. Sales training today needs to emphasize listening skills and consultative selling. It's called the 'new authenticity' and it simply means being real with your customers."

"Listening! How hard is that? Don't you just stop talking?" asked Zack.

"You'd be surprised, Zack. It's a paradox of sales. Organizations hire people with extremely outgoing personalities and fantastic verbal skills. These same people are then expected to demonstrate great listening skills. It's difficult, but with training and experience, these seemingly contradictory skills can coexist. Many people in management don't appreciate the difficulty of developing speaking and listening skills simultaneously. Most people are born without a high degree of skill in both listening and speaking. You have to master the mental balancing act of doing both at the same time to be a true sales professional. For most sales professionals it is a learned skill.

"While we're on training, I'd like to make a few comments about how organizations approach sales training and why it doesn't have as much impact as it could. Think about a typical sales hierarchy, CEO – President – V.P. of Sales – Regional Sales Directors – Sales Managers – Sales force. Sales skills training is usually directed at the sales force, the lowest level. Companies will spend large amounts of money on internally and/or externally generated sales training without ever validating with sales management that it is reinforcing their sales goals and objectives. The tactic is to simply throw some generic sales training at the sales force and hope it somehow helps. What's even worse is that the training is viewed as a seed. Plant it one time and it will grow into a great big money tree. That is not reality. Training has to be continuous in order to reinforce prior training. Ongoing

The Productive Employee

training is necessary as business environments and industries inevitably change.

"Imagine someone dressed in the best looking football uniform money can buy with all the latest protective equipment. Imagine this person is one of the most highly motivated individuals on the planet and has dreamed of playing with the NFL all his life. He's young and incredibly physically fit as well. It has been his life's goal to play professional football. He would sacrifice anything to achieve his dream. There is one problem, however. Other than many years of pick-up football games and intramural play in college, he's never had any professional coaching. What are the chances he'll be picked up by the NFL? Zero. What's missing? Skills training. Even with an incredible amount of innate talent, he would never succeed in a game that requires such a multitude of learned skills. A company cannot simply hire motivated employees, provide the best tools available and expect great things to happen from that point forward. Even if they hire someone who has 'prior experience' from other jobs, we all know that no two companies operate in the same way. On top of that, prior experience can become stale very quickly."

Comatose Management

"Okay, I think I understand. A complete and effective employee will be motivated, have the right tools and be well trained."

"You are right, except you are leaving out the final and most complex variable. I think we would all agree that working hard with the right tools and having the necessary skills are fundamental to employee productivity, not to mention employee satisfaction. There is one final variable that ties motivation, tools and abilities together. I can best explain this final variable with a mathematical formula. I'll write the following formula on a napkin for you."

$$I(M + S + T) = Productivity$$

"What do the letters mean?" asked Zack.

"'M' indicates 'motivation,' 'S' signifies 'skills' and 'T' designates 'tools.' 'I' specifies 'intelligence.' Think about it Zack. A person's innate intelligence will obviously affect how far his or her skills can be developed through training and experience. It will also influence his or her motivation. The more intelligent a person is the more this person understands how his or her ambition, or lack of, will affect career success. Someone who has an above average intelligence will use tools more effectively and efficiently than

The Productive Employee

the average person will. This is as true today as it was with the 19th century blacksmith. Let me rewrite the formula in another way algebraically, although the result will be the same."

$$(I \times M) + (I \times S) + (I \times T) = Productivity$$

"All I am saying, Zack, is that natural intelligence either amplifies or decreases each of the components of employee productivity we've been talking about. This is not a particularly *popular* variable because we don't like to talk about differences in intelligence between people. We certainly are not allowed to test for it when we hire someone. There is a large army of psychologists and educators who believe IQ tests don't accurately indicate a person's intelligence anyway. One of the most perplexing things about intelligence, as opposed to the other three variables, is that an employer can't alter how smart someone is, or isn't. A good boss, great working environment, pay raises, etc. can frequently improve an employee's motivation. The best and latest tools can be provided to an employee. Skills can be enhanced through experience and instruction; the amount of training an employee receives is only limited by time and budgets. However, we haven't learned how to make someone genetically smarter."

Comatose Management

Zack asked, "If we can't make someone more intelligent or test for it, do we even need to worry about it?"

"Yes, we do need to worry about it because, as I have said, it affects everything else."

"What can an employer do about it?"

"Employers can best match a candidate with a job *before* he or she is hired. When hiring, they need to be careful to verify that the applicant has actually performed the job he or she is being interviewed for in a similar environment to the one the employer will provide. They can also closely evaluate an applicant's verbal skills during the interview process. It is my belief, and that of many others, that verbal skills are a prima facie indicator of intellect.

"If the employer ultimately makes a hiring mismatch, they can adjust for the error by moving the individual into a more appropriate position if they realize the new employee is in over his or her head. They also need to be vigilant about moving people into positions that are more cerebral when employees aren't being adequately challenged.

"The funny thing about intelligence is that even though it's illegal to test for IQ, it's markedly obvious to almost everyone, fairly quickly, when someone doesn't pack the mental muscle power needed for a job or when someone isn't being adequately challenged."

The Productive Employee

"Don't most employers know to weigh and monitor these variables when hiring and developing employees?" asked Zack.

"It would seem they would, but most don't. They either don't know to do this or are unwilling to make the effort. Employers of all sizes usually tend to view employees as one-dimensional. They don't realize that people are salads made up of many different parts. Change one thing and the salad can taste awful. I love salads, but put anchovies in mine and I'm not going to get along with it. Anchovies are a non-starter for me. When companies hire someone, they typically are only interested in the answer to the following question, 'Do we perceive this person can do the job?' You'll notice that this question is a closed ended question, which means it can be answered with one word. This is not enough information to make a hiring and placement decision. People are more complicated than that. In fact, people are downright messy, with hundreds, maybe thousands, of additional variables we haven't even touched on. Employers should be looking under every rock accessible to them in order to discover an applicant's motivation, skill levels and perceived intelligence."

"Is it important to ask how much training a job candidate has had at past jobs?" Zack asked.

Comatose Management

"I really don't care how much training someone has had historically. What I care about is his or her current skill level. The candidate may have had thousands of hours of training, but if his or her skill levels are poor, it could indicate problems with motivation during training, ability to comprehend the training (intelligence) or even inferior training. The quality of past training and a person's comprehension of it will be reflected in his or her ability to demonstrate what he or she knows. As an employer, I should be interested in training in the future tense, not the past tense. What training am I going to provide for new employees to help them develop, based on where they are now and where I need them to be?

"Companies continually make the same mistakes when hiring and developing employees. They tend to treat all people the same, as if everyone had the same skills, IQ and motivation. Experience tells us people are like snowflakes. No two are the same. Everyone brings a different bag of tricks to the table and we must adjust accordingly. Not only does this produce better training and development results, but it is more cost effective as well.

"This same one-dimensional view of employees carries through to evaluations too. Most companies perform an obligatory annual review

The Productive Employee

of all their employees. This in itself is funny if you think about it. They review their employees once a *year*! Doesn't seem like quite enough to me. Can you imagine only checking in with your strategic customers once a year? On top of that, most companies use the same evaluation process (i.e., form) to evaluate all of their employees regardless of level or function. They may have used this same process for the last 30+ years. In *progressive* companies you'll occasionally see two forms used during evaluations, one for 'management' and one for 'others.' Of course I'm kidding about the 'progressive' part.

"I believe, Zack, that most companies have some awareness of the complexity of the people they hire and put on their payrolls. But, looking at people as individuals, with all their variables, takes too much effort and time. It's easier to see everyone as an 'employee' instead of a person. Any time you take a custom approach to anything it is more difficult and takes more time. Whenever we do, however, we usually get a better product and one that comes closer to meeting our needs.

"Zack, let's get a refill on our coffee. Oh, I forgot, you have to pay for refills here don't you? I hate that about Starbucks."

4
CAPTAIN NEPOTISM

⌘ ⌘ ⌘

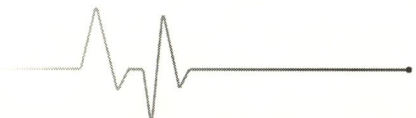

"Zack, I understand you are considering going to work at your uncle's company. Did you know that I have spent a large portion of my career working in family-owned businesses?"

Nothing is more real than the lessons we learn from our life experiences and I sure have learned a thing or two about family-owned businesses. People frequently ask me if they should work for a family member who owns his or her own business. I always give them the same advice. There are studies showing that only about 10% of family-owned businesses survive from one generation to the next. Most of them are managed by emotion rather than logic and are inefficient because of all the bizarre family dynamics. Many families

Comatose Management

are destroyed by working together; the list is virtually endless. Everyone thinks they will be the exception. I tell them, find another place to work.

"Zack, you must be very careful before deciding to work for your family. Allow me to tell you a story about a friend of mine who went to work in a family owned business. He was not a family member, but his observations are noteworthy."

Martin Koln could hardly sleep last night; today is his first day on the job. He grew up with Tim Jatterson, whose father owns Jatterson Plumbing Supply. Tim hooked Martin up with a job at his dad's company. He was not exactly sure what he would be doing there, but the important thing was that he had a job.

Martin had finished high school and had completed 30 hours at a local junior college while working at a local Ford dealership in their parts department. He was 23. One might be tempted to think that Martin was only moderately intelligent and had limited career aspirations based on his quiet nature. Those assumptions would be very incorrect, however. Martin was the kind of person who was going to be successful no matter what he did in his life. He had graduated in the top 5% of his high school class and breezed through his junior college classes. He thought junior college

Captain Nepotism

was easier than high school. He made A's and B's in every class.

He also liked leading teams. He was a natural leader. Martin was one of those oddballs who was both the manager of his varsity baseball team and the President of his chess club in high school. He was well liked. Tim Jatterson was his best friend.

Martin was very nervous when he walked in the front door of Jatterson Plumbing Supply. He looked around the entryway and did not see Tim. It was probably a little naïve of him to think that Tim would be waiting there for him. Jatterson was housed in a building that Martin estimated was built around 1950. It was clean and functional he thought. For work, he certainly did not need anything fancy. What Martin cared most about was an opportunity to move up the corporate ladder and make lots of money.

The receptionist looked at Martin and said, "May I help you?" It seemed odd that she did not recognize him despite the fact that he was now an employee there.

"I'm Martin Koln. I am starting work today and I am supposed to report to Wayne Humphries."

Wayne Humphries was some sort of manager in the warehouse who was not related to the Jatterson family in any way. Martin felt a little disappointed that he was not going to immediately report to a

Comatose Management

Jatterson family member. It seemed like he could progress a little faster in the organization if he were connected with one of the family members. He figured that he would have to pay his dues though, and this was just part of it.

"Wayne Humphries, you have a visitor in the reception area," was announced at least twice by the receptionist over the intercom system. It did not make Martin feel very special. Martin waited in a chair in the reception area and started to see some things he did not like about the building he was going to be working in. Why was he being so critical? He noticed how the faded artificial plants looked like they were older than he was and really needed to be dusted. The carpeting was badly worn where people rested their feet while sitting in the reception area chairs.

"Hi! You must be Martin Koln!" announced a man who was obviously Wayne Humphries. Wayne thrust his hand out and gave Martin's a good hard shake. Martin was happy to finally be connected with someone who knew he was supposed to be there. There was something about Wayne that bothered Martin a little bit. Wayne was in his late forties, slightly bald, short and wore clothes that looked like they were from Goodwill. Martin did not care anything about clothes, but there was

Captain Nepotism

something about Wayne that bothered him. He could not figure out what it was.

Martin thanked the receptionist and followed Wayne back to the warehouse. As Martin was following Wayne, it dawned on him that he was going to be working in the warehouse. It was not exactly what he had in mind, but he was adaptable and knew he had to start somewhere. What kind of boss was Wayne going to be? Did Wayne know that he was Tim's best friend? Tim *Jatterson's* best friend.

Wayne pointed to a loading dock area and said, "See all those boxes? Those are filled with valves that need to be moved over to this high rack area. They are heavy. Are you up to some heavy lifting?"

Martin was physically more than able to move the valves. He was happy to have something to do, to be honest. He calculated that there were over 300 boxes and it would take him the better part of the morning to get them moved and on the shelves. About halfway through this project, he heard a familiar voice from behind; it was Tim.

Tim looked different to Martin. He was wearing nicer clothes than anyone in the warehouse and he had a clipboard with important looking paperwork clipped to it. Tim even treated Martin differently it seemed. He spoke to Martin

Comatose Management

in a more official capacity, almost as if they didn't know one another. It bothered Martin.

"How are things going so far?"

"I'm off to a good start," Martin replied.

"Well, you're in good hands with old Wayne," said Tim, "He has been with us for over 20 years." After that brief exchange, Tim quickly left the warehouse. Martin realized he had just been given a courtesy call by his best friend.

Martin began thinking about what Tim said about Wayne. 20 years! How could anyone work anywhere for 20 years and end up as a warehouse manager? Martin figured that Wayne Humphries was either not very smart or just not very motivated; otherwise, he would have been in a high-level management position at Jatterson Plumbing.

Around 9:30 a.m., Wayne walked through the warehouse and announced to all the warehouse employees that it was break time. "Time for beak, time for break, time for break," he said. Martin sat down in a designated break area with the other warehouse employees. He looked around and saw about 25 other warehouse workers. He felt a little odd as the other employees stared at him, so he took the initiative and introduced himself. Had no one announced a new person was going to be starting? Seems like someone should have let

Captain Nepotism

the other employees know there would be a new employee.

Just as Martin was introducing himself to about the 14th person, he noticed there was a window that opened into what looked like the general office area. It was a small window and Martin figured it was put there years ago for office people to monitor the warehouse workers. Even though just a wall and some glass separated the warehouse from the office area, there was a world of difference in what he saw.

The area on the other side of the glass had a different color paint, was completely carpeted (although somewhat worn looking like the carpeting in the reception area), had lots of dark veneer office furniture and many faded fake plants (also like the ones in the reception area). Everyone on the other side of the window seemed to be dressed nicely, similar to the way Tim was dressed when he saw him earlier. Martin guessed there were 15 or more people in the front office. That was obviously the part of the building where management resided.

Trying to make small talk, Martin looked at one of the people he just met (but had forgotten her name already) and said, "Who are all of those people in the office?"

Comatose Management

The woman answered with a question that surprised him. "Oh, do you mean the Jatterson Jillions?" Martin had no idea what she meant.

"What are the Jatterson Jillions?" he said.

"Oh you don't know yet, do you? Well, they are all of the chiefs that really matter at this company. Some of them even have a car that is paid for by the company. Must be nice!"

Just about that time Martin saw Tim through the window and said to this woman, "Do you know Tim Jatterson? He is my best friend and helped me get this job."

"Of course, everyone knows Tim. He is the Executive Senior Vice President of Special Projects. His daddy owns the place and the two of them are the two big bosses here." When Martin asked her more about what Tim's job responsibilities were, the woman was not able to answer. She just knew he was important.

Break time was over and Martin was even more curious about what Tim did at Jatterson. He was also curious to know more about the other people he saw through the window. He was just finishing his job of moving the valves when a loud buzzer sounded, which he was told indicated that the lunch hour was starting. Martin had no lunch plans; he was wondering if Wayne, or maybe even Tim, would invite him to lunch.

Captain Nepotism

"Are you ready for lunch, Martin?" shouted Tim from across the warehouse. Martin was relieved he had someone to go to lunch with and it was going to be his best friend, Tim. "Everyone in the front office…including my dad…are all going to go to lunch today for a lunch meeting. I asked if you could go too and my dad said it was fine with him." Martin did not know whether he was a tag along or whether it was an honor to be included. Nonetheless, he was invited and would get to meet all of those people on the other side of the window.

Martin walked with Tim to the office area and found the same 15 front office people standing around, apparently waiting to go to lunch. Martin saw Tim's dad, Bill, across the room and walked up to him to say hello. Martin had called Tim's dad by his first name since Martin turned 20. When he spoke to him that day he called him "Bill" as he had been doing for the last few years. Suddenly the office got completely quiet. Martin knew something had just happened that was not good, but he did not know what it was or if he had caused it. He looked around and noticed no one was making eye contact with him and everyone was primarily looking at the floor. Tim rushed over to Martin and whispered to him, "Everyone but family members calls my dad Mr. Jatterson."

Comatose Management

Martin was both embarrassed and confused at the same time. He was humiliated because he had made such a major mistake in his first half day on the job. Did there need to be a different relationship between Bill and Martin because Bill was the owner, or simply because Martin was not a Jatterson family member?

Martin wanted to understand more about the Jatterson family mystique so he asked, "Tim, how many of these front office people are family members?"

Tim's response was simple and terrifying at the same time, "All of them." Tim laughed when Martin asked him if he needed to call all of the family members by their last name. "The only person you need to call Mr. Jatterson is my dad," he said. Martin looked around and saw there were several people who looked to be his age in the front office. Were these people managers too? Does the Jatterson name mean you own the keys to the kingdom, regardless of age, background or experience?

During lunch, Martin started to learn a lot about "the family." There were 15 management people in the front office and just as Tim had said, literally every single one of them was related to Mr. Jatterson in some way. There were brothers, sisters, nieces, nephews, aunts, uncles and even an

Captain Nepotism

ex-spouse. Throughout the entire lunch, everyone seemed to stare at Mr. Jatterson and kept a smile on their face the entire time. Whenever Mr. Jatterson spoke, everyone immediately ceded the floor to him and listened attentively. Whenever Mr. Jatterson made anything even resembling a joke, everyone laughed. They seemed to talk a lot about lake houses, new cars, boats and private schools. It became clear to Martin that he was around the decision makers at Jatterson Plumbing Supply.

Mr. Jatterson picked up the tab for lunch, of course, and everyone seemed to go a little overboard in thanking him for his generosity. Martin thought, if this was some kind of front office meeting there was not much business transacted. It didn't matter; Martin got a free lunch and got to learn a little bit more about how things really work at Jatterson.

When Martin returned to the warehouse, the first thing Wayne did was to look at his watch. He did not say anything, but the message was loud and clear. Martin was surprised when Wayne asked him, "Are you related to the Jattersons in any way?" Martin told him he was not. "Very unusual for an outsider to go to lunch with the Jatterson Jillions," said Wayne. There was that term again.

Comatose Management

"What exactly does everyone mean when they say Jatterson Jillions?" asked Martin.

"The Jatterson Jillions are all the family members who work here, and there are a *jillion* of them, let me tell you. It also represents the kind of money they make. You and I will never make the kind of money they make. Get used to it boy. I have been here over 20 years and I am just glad to have the job. I'm not blood so I should not expect to have what they have. The fact is, I am the highest-level management employee here who is not blood so I feel good about that. I have a brother I could have gotten a job here but he was not interested. He wanted to go to work for a *public* company, whatever that means. He was not smart enough to take advantage of the opportunity to work for a family company. We are all family here, even if you are not a Jatterson. The Jattersons are very proud of that fact."

"We are all one of two groups here," would have been a more accurate statement to Martin. Either you were "in" or you were "out" of the family. If Wayne Humphries was the highest-level non-family member, then clearly, being an outsider was not the road to riches and career success at Jatterson Plumbing Supply.

Martin reflected back on his math courses from junior college. He recalled that everything

Captain Nepotism

in life had a bell curve. Extremes of good and bad had limited numbers with most things being average. Most people were of average intelligence with only a handful being bright and a handful being somewhat slow. It seemed unlikely to Martin that all of Bill Jatterson's relatives were going to be on the brightest side of that bell curve. It was impossible that one family would harbor nothing but brilliant and talented people. As much as he liked Tim as a friend, he never thought of him as supremely bright. Tim relied on Martin to help him with his homework all through high school. It didn't make sense. Even though they were the same age and Martin had more education and smarts, Tim had an office in the front and Martin was in the warehouse moving boxes around.

While Martin continued to work, he had a lot of time to think about this situation. All 15 of the front office managers, the people that were really running the company from what he could tell, were somehow related to Mr. Jatterson. Martin was very capable in math and the next formula he contrived barely challenged him at all mathematically, but alarmed him from a career perspective. He thought to himself, the highest level I can ever hope to achieve in this company could be represented by a math formula.

Comatose Management

Highest Level Achievable = (number of Jatterson relatives) + 1. Wayne Humphries is number 16 at Jatterson Plumbing Supply since he is the highest-level non-family employee. To get to number 16 I would have to unseat Wayne Humphries, who has been here over 20 years.

Reality was starting to come crashing in on Martin. He was not having a good first day. This was not a career company; this was just an earn-a-paycheck company - unless you were related to Mr. Jatterson. Jobs like this can be good, but not when you are young, motivated, intelligent and not a family member.

Martin thought of himself as a physically strong person, but after all the heavy lifting he was not so sure about that anymore. He saw some of the older and frailer looking people throwing boxes around with greater ease. He figured it must be an issue of technique versus raw strength.

As Martin was moving the boxes of valves, he continued to process the things he was beginning to realize. While the Jatterson family members seemed to be nice and Tim was his best friend, none of them had ever struck him as highly motivated or intelligent. Did Mr. Jatterson have a rule that he would only select family members for significant management positions? In a smallish

Captain Nepotism

family owned business, did they really need 15 front office management types? Did Mr. Jatterson create these jobs just so he could employ his family members? While that was a nice gesture on his part, Martin had to wonder if there were better employees he could have hired from the "outside." He didn't hire outsiders because they did not meet the Jatterson directive of being a family member. Were there candidates for even the warehouse positions who would not be interested in working for Jatterson Plumbing Supply because they realized the same thing Martin did, $15 + 1 = 16$?

Martin started to get a little angry. Part of it was because he was really starting to sweat as he continued to work. The other reason was that he realized his career opportunities were limited at Jatterson Plumbing Supply, no matter how well he performed. He even thought to himself, why should I work my tail off here? It will make no difference. And, what kind of people am I going to be working around? Are they people who don't realize they will not ever go anywhere in this company or are happy to work with a management team that, by the power of the bell curve, cannot be the best and the brightest? The pool of smart management candidates from the Jatterson family just cannot be that big. That limits the potential for the success of Jatterson as a company and

Comatose Management

especially limits career opportunities for non-Jatterson employees.

Martin wondered how all of this happened. How did a small to medium sized company end up with 15 family members in management, 25 non-family warehouse workers and 35 salespeople? After subtly asking around at his next break, Martin learned that none of the 35 salespeople were related to the Jattersons. Why was that?

Martin's dad sold bricks to the building industry. He remembered his dad saying many times at the dinner table, "Martin, there are three groups of people in the business world. Salesmen are those who can bring revenue into a company and are the most valued. There are those outside of sales who work 8 to 5 in the home office. Finally, those who cannot do either, train salespeople." Martin's dad died when he was only 48. He remembered his dad working hard for what seemed like not very much money. Sales is a difficult career path and it took its toll on Martin's dad. "Either you make your number in sales or you don't. You've got it or you don't," Martin's dad used to say. To Martin this explained why there were no Jatterson relatives in sales at Jatterson Plumbing Supply.

Captain Nepotism

Martin did an inventory of the employment situation at Jatterson Plumbing and realized these truths:

1. First, he was, at best, only going to be able to rise to a position that was one more numerically than the total number of Jatterson relatives. A person with significant capabilities and career ambitions would not find that kind of limitation particularly appealing.
2. He thought giving family members the best jobs in the company did not exactly motivate those within the company to try harder. This would apply to non-Jatterson employees *and* Jatterson relatives. With such an absolute career ceiling, there was little motivation for the non-Jatterson employees to strive to do their best.
3. There were probably many positions in the company that had been created so relatives could have jobs. These would have been high paying jobs too, which seemed only to make things worse in Martin's opinion. Overpaying people to be in positions that are created for them is destructive to the business in all kinds of ways.

4. He felt Mr. Jatterson was greatly limiting his talent pool by only selecting candidates from Jatterson relatives. The Jatterson family just was not that big; compromises had to be made somewhere. A company needs to find the best employees it can in order to survive and prosper. This scenario almost guarantees that will not happen.
5. He now better understood why Wayne Humphries' brother was not interested in working for Jatterson Plumbing. There is no place to go. A potential contributor never even got out of the gate.
6. Since it appeared to Martin that Mr. Jatterson handed out the best jobs to his relatives, they were all beholden to him. They had to know they could not get jobs like this outside of the family business. How does this affect their confidence levels and effectiveness? Mr. Jatterson's new clothes were always quite beautiful and his jokes the funniest. Mr. Jatterson was not getting good business intelligence from his family members, nor was he seeing assertiveness that is needed in business.
7. Martin realized that, over time, Jatterson Plumbing Supply had collected relatives who were overpaid and/or over their heads in

Captain Nepotism

their jobs. Simultaneously, they amassed a group of non-relatives who were not smart enough to see the lack of a career path and/or were unmotivated enough not to mind. An employee complement of overpaid and unmotivated employees can only make a company less competitive and less profitable.
8. He realized that the Jattersons ate together, played together, went to church together and, since they were related, many of them lived together. There seemed to be a chronic shortage of new ideas or fresh thinking. There were no outside influences, good or bad. Martin heard several times on his first day, "There is a right way, there is a wrong way and there is Mr. Jatterson's way." While Jatterson Plumbing Supply had few new ideas coming in, their no-nepotism competitors were looking for and getting them from their employees.

Martin realized that while Mr. Jatterson viewed his family members as contributors and his hiring of them as altruistic, they were damaging his business in many more ways than he would ever know.

Martin's dad never went very far as a brick salesperson. Martin was determined not to end up in a nowhere job like his dad. The main reason he went to work for Tim Jatterson's dad was that he thought it would help get his career off to a fast start. He was beginning to realize that the very thing he thought was going to get his career revved up was setting him on a path to do just the opposite. He did not want to be a Wayne Humphries.

Then it dawned on Martin what it was that bothered him about Wayne when he first met him. Wayne looked like the building. Wayne's general worn out appearance seemed to perfectly match the worn out appearance of the building that housed Jatterson Plumbing Supply. Wayne had *become* Jatterson Plumbing Supply. He was number 16, happy to be there, and blended in even more than he realized, except for one thing. He was not a Jatterson and never would be.

"Zack, I'm glad we're friends and I don't want to see you hurt your career, so I hope you will think long and hard before jumping into a family business. Your uncle may be a great guy at family gatherings, but working for him might not be the best idea."

5

ONLY A MAN CAN MANAGE

⌘ ⌘ ⌘

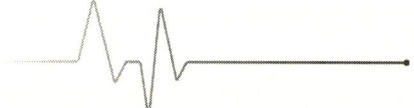

"**G**ood morning Zack. Someone gave me a gift card. Coffee is on me today. Make it a Venti.

"So, your new boss is a woman? Have you ever worked for a woman? I have to tell you, Zack, that some of the most capable management people I know are women. I have worked with, and for, some of the best in my career. I see businesses every day that would not even exist if it were not for their female management. I also see too many businesses that unfortunately will never see women as legitimate candidates for significant management positions. When choosing to safeguard the idea that only men can lead,

Comatose Management

companies severely limit their management pool. Do you have time for a story, Zack?"

"Sure."

I began my story.

After spending the last five years with Carter Fluid Power, a manufacturer of fluid power products, Elizabeth knew a thing or two about hydraulics and pneumatics. It took her five years to get to a point where she would even consider interviewing for a new job outside of Carter Fluid Power. She was aware there were some risks in interviewing for a job while currently employed, but she also knew she had become an expert in fluid power products and felt confident she could quickly find another job before her current employer found out.

Why was she considering interviewing?

Elizabeth was a member of the engineering club in college and was not the first to notice that there seemed to be two types of people in the engineering club: guys and not-so-pretty girls. She may not have been very pretty by most people's standards, but she was considered quite gifted by all of her college professors. She double majored in mechanical and electrical engineering. Her faculty advisor practically begged her to enroll in the graduate program, but she was tired of school by then. She opted for a job right out of college at a large pneumatics manufacturer, Carter Fluid Power.

She was almost embarrassed to admit it initially, but Elizabeth loved pneumatic valves and fittings right from the start. She was able to quickly grasp the concept of how everything fit into the big picture. Her first job was in customer pre-sales support. Since ninety percent of their sales were to distributors, she primarily dealt with that arena but enjoyed working with end-users better. She was not particularly impressed with the technical abilities of some of the distributors, but many of the big end-users had some real engineering horsepower in her estimation. It was not long until head technicians and engineers from many of Carter's customers were calling her for advice. Even more surprising to her was that she knew the answers and they were using her suggestions. She knew she was in the right industry.

She enjoyed being able to provide customers with the information they needed and getting to know them at the same time. She found it frustrating at times when the Carter Fluid Power sales representatives would get involved in her communications with customers. Sometimes they helped, and sometimes they did not, but they were always happy to have her technical expertise available to assist them in making the sale. She

Comatose Management

got along very well with not only the customers, but also the Carter sales representatives as well. She felt blessed to have a job she enjoyed while simultaneously being able to help others do their jobs better.

However, Elizabeth was feeling an extra helping of blessings at this time that had nothing to do with pneumatics. She had met someone at her church she was romantically interested in. His name was Tim Southern. The best news was that Tim was interested in her too. They had even danced around the idea of marriage and discussed having a family together.

They had been dating for almost six months when the President of Carter asked Elizabeth and her boss to come into his office. The President, Ralph Kaperson, did all the talking. He had the largest office in the company and it had big executive looking dark furniture that was the nicest in the building. Elizabeth naturally assumed he was the most capable and knowledgeable leader in the company. He asked her if she would be interested in being the manager of customer service. In short, Carter Fluid Power wanted to give her a promotion. Elizabeth immediately jumped to her feet and said, "Sure!" There were a few moments of embarrassing silence. She did not realize she

Only a Man Can Manage

would have to go through a formal internal interview process in order to officially get the job. It would be the kind of interview that is done because corporations are supposed to do formal internal interviews, not because they serve any real purpose. After the dust of that little faux pas passed, they all agreed on a time when the President and Elizabeth's current boss would get together for an official internal interview. It was scheduled for the next day at 3:00 p.m.

When Elizabeth entered the conference room for her interview she found eight other people in the room. She noticed her boss and the President, but she also saw the warehouse manager, inventory control manager, office manager, building maintenance manager, quality control manager and the President's assistant. Everyone in the room, except for Elizabeth and the President's assistant, was a man. That struck her as a little odd. It also struck her as a little peculiar that all of the additional managers in the room had little to do with customer service. She didn't want to seem snobby about it, but she realized they were all lower ranking managers as well. This did not feel right to Elizabeth, but she wanted the promotion and would endure whatever interview protocols were customary at Carter. She had come prepared to talk about her customer successes and her plans

Comatose Management

for improving Carter's customer service even further.

Ralph Kaperson, the company President, started out by saying, "Thank you for meeting with us today to discuss the customer service supervisor position." Elizabeth thought to herself, I was told this was for the customer service *manager*, not supervisor, position. Mr. Kaperson continued, "We should go ahead and begin the interviewing. John, as warehouse manager, do you have any questions?"

"Yes I do, Mr. Kaperson. Elizabeth could you tell us about your participation in sports teams in school or in adult leagues?" Elizabeth frankly did not know what the warehouse manager was doing in the room in the first place and was further confused with his first question. Maybe he was just trying to warm things up a bit. He was probably a bright person or he wouldn't be a manager.

"I can't say that I ever really participated in formal athletic events. I was very involved in social clubs and academic organizations, but not organized athletics." The warehouse manager looked concerned and motioned that he had no further questions.

Mr. Kaperson then motioned to his assistant to continue the questioning. His assistant was 27

Only a Man Can Manage

years old and a winner at some beauty contest in a small southern city when she was 21. The beauty contest had something to do with peaches. She was a beautiful woman in every way. "Do you understand the Internet and email and things such as that? I struggled with those things for a long time when I first started at Carter until Ralph…Mr. Kaperson…showed me how all those computer things worked."

Elizabeth was embarrassed for Miss Peach for three reasons: 1. That she asked such a dumb question, 2. That Miss Peach did not know to be embarrassed, and 3. That the President of Carter would have an assistant as incompetent as Miss Peach appeared to be.

Elizabeth answered the question in the best way she knew how, "yes."

Next up was the office manager. Sally was a schoolteacher for many years before coming to work at Carter. Mr. Kaperson relied on Sally for everything around the office that, ironically, did not involve actually running the office. Most of the employees at Carter wondered why Sally had been put in charge of office management; she seemed to have few skills related to actually running an office. As a result, she had become the self-appointed queen of furniture, floral arrangements, cubicle assignments, wall color, building maintenance and exterior landscaping at Carter. By this time, Elizabeth was bracing herself for the next irrelevant question. "Elizabeth, have you ever been involved with the PTA?"

Since Elizabeth had never been married and had no children this seemed like an easy one to answer. "I have no children and as a result have never been involved in any kind of PTA organization."

Sally's expression immediately intensified and she asked, "You've never been married? You're a smart and capable girl and it seems there would be a lot of men who would be interested in you." Sally looked at the rest of the group and smiled. There was no way in the world that Elizabeth intended to tell them anything about Tim or anything else in her personal life. What in the world did the PTA or being single have to do with her getting a promotion to customer service manager, or supervisor, or whatever they were going to call this position? Elizabeth came to this interview expecting to bond with her new peer managers, but instead was feeling increasingly alienated.

After a series of additional questions that had nothing to do with either customer service or management, Mr. Kaperson finally said,

Only a Man Can Manage

"I have one final question for you before we conclude this interview. As you know, fluid power products can be a tough industry. You have to be able to operate and compete in a man's world to be successful. Sometimes you might have to get dirt under your fingernails and, at the same time, you might have to put on a nice dress for our bigger customers. Each of our customers will view our customer service area differently and you have to be as flexible as a man would be in the same position. We feel confident in offering you the customer service lead position, if you feel you can operate in that kind of environment. We wish we had more women helping us manage this company, but the reality is that the pool of candidates is small and men just naturally tend to take charge of things in this business. The promotion also includes something that will definitely get your attention, a 3.25% raise; I almost forgot to mention that. I'm sure you could use the extra money. Let us know tomorrow if you are interested in accepting the lead position we've discussed today."

Five years of solid performance at Carter Fluid Power and the company President structures an internal interview with the following attributes:

Comatose Management

- No female managers were involved. Carter did not have any to pick from anyway, so this really was a non-issue in an odd kind of way.
- The questions that were asked dealt with Elizabeth's gender and not her job knowledge and skills.
- None of the managers who truly affected customer service were even in the room during the interview.
- Obviously the company was gun-shy about calling Elizabeth a "manager," so they continually dumbed down the job description, manager – supervisor – lead.

Elizabeth realized she had become a victim of the "you-gotta-be-a-man-to-manage" mentality. That concept really turned her off. She naively thought she would never have to deal with that in her career. However, it was real after all and she had become a participant in the game. By giving her a real promotion to manager they would have to violate too many rules of the game. These violations would include:

- She is not a man.
- She does not understand men's social protocols.
- Women are not allowed in legitimate management positions.

Only a Man Can Manage

- The manufacturing and distribution industries are a "man's world" and not fit for women, nor can women prosper in them.
- Women are not genetically predisposed to management.
- Promoting a woman who is clearly more intelligent than many of the current male managers, including the company President, could upset the social order.
- God put women on earth primarily to bear children. That must be respected above everything else.

Clearly, Elizabeth was half-heartedly being offered a lightweight promotion. It seemed when she first started talking with Mr. Kaperson that she would be interviewing for a manager position and now he seemed almost hesitant about offering her a *lead* position. What made Mr. Kaperson bring up the possible promotion in the first place and why had he reduced it to a *lead* position? Why was he playing this game? Carter Fluid Power had almost 250 employees and there were only four women supervisors. No women could be found in management above the supervisor level. Those four women all supervised women in the credit and order entry departments. Was Mr. Kaperson trying to introduce additional female "management"

Comatose Management

into Carter? Did he think he was going to lose Elizabeth if he didn't give her some kind of promotion?

After five years of working at Carter, Elizabeth saw the management structure for what it was. It was male dominated and those male managers were not the best and brightest available. She did not need to be a math whiz to realize that when you eliminate more than fifty-percent of the population (there are more women in the world than men), the selection becomes a lot leaner and one has to "settle" for what one can get. For that matter, she realized that many of the companies she worked with were organized the same way. Men ran the show and women were given token management jobs in clerical areas. Was this not how it was done back in the 1950's? Has it changed that little?

Elizabeth joined Tim later that evening for dinner and told him everything. In fact, about halfway through the evening she realized she had probably told him more details than he wanted to know. He was always complaining about that issue with her. Tim would say, "Elizabeth, just give me the bottom line and I'll help you work this out." He was very understanding that evening and managed to listen to her entire story. His advice to her was simple and straightforward, and mostly unsolicited.

Only a Man Can Manage

"So what if there are only a couple of women in supervisory roles at Carter? This is your chance to help even things up. You are one of the smartest women at Carter and you'll help women more by taking the job rather than not taking it. This is a chance for you to show them what you can really do and maybe be considered for additional promotions." It all seemed very simple to Tim. Elizabeth thanked him for listening, paid her half of the check at Bennigan's and drove herself home.

The next morning at work, she checked with Miss Peach and found that Mr. Kaperson was in his office. She proudly walked into his big office containing piles of paperwork that had not been moved in years (so Mr. Kaperson looked busy) and told him she would accept the new position being offered to her. Mr. Kaperson stood up, smiled, shook her hand (limply) and said, "I knew you would take it and I'm glad. This position is too good for a girl with your experience to pass up. Get with my assistant and she'll get the paperwork started."

A "girl" can only take so much condescension and patronization.

Elizabeth immediately got in her car and drove to the nearest Starbucks where she started contacting recruiters. She realized she was having a Rosa Parks moment. She was tired of this

Comatose Management

treatment and was going to take action, even if it meant setbacks. It was time for her to go and she was somewhat upset with herself for waiting five years to do so. She was not working with smart people or progressive thinkers at any level and she finally acknowledged what she had been denying for many years. Her career opportunities were limited at Carter.

She had to be careful to think this through in a way that was not driven by anger. Angry decision-making is poor decision making. It was difficult for her to realize that not only was she working in an environment that was biased against women, but the management of the company, which was essentially 100% male, was not very competent. It took this incident for her to realize that being a man with a title does not guarantee capability.

She had been applying at all the web-based job sites when she realized she did not even have a current resume. She closed her laptop, finished her latte and went back to work. The next day she was amazed and encouraged to see that by noon she had 37 personal emails from companies indicating interest in talking with her. She was able to immediately dismiss most of them because they were for insurance or vitamin sales positions, but there were three of them that looked promising on the surface. Two of the three positions listed a salary level that was $10,000 more per year than she was currently making, even with her "generous" 3.25% raise factored in.

One of the most promising jobs she saw was with a company that was already one of her customers, a medium-sized distributor of fluid power products located less than ten miles from her home. After a series of phone calls and emails, they were able to connect and Elizabeth got an interview with the VP of Sales, Stephen Deen. She was a little concerned that since this was a customer of Carter Fluid Products word might get back that she was interviewing with them. She dismissed this concern because most companies these days adhere to strict rules of confidentiality in order to avoid litigation.

When she arrived at Enterprise Fluid Power Products for her interview, she was astonished to realize the receptionist used the old pink slips to keep track of messages. Who uses those any more? As she walked into the reception area, and before she had time to introduce herself, the receptionist picked up one of the pink slips and read it aloud to a man walking by. She said, "Bill, Stephen Deen has an interview with someone from Carter Fluid Power that he doesn't have time to talk to today. Would you have time to give her a courtesy interview?" Bill simply grabbed the pink slip from

Comatose Management

her without saying a word and walked down the hall. The receptionist looked at Elizabeth and said, "Can I help you?"

With the information she had just gained, Elizabeth answered by saying, "I was to have an interview with Stephen Deen in 10 minutes."

Without blinking an eye, the receptionist said, "Oh, I'm so sorry. Mr. Deen had a sudden emergency and will not be talking with you today, but we've scheduled someone else to see you." She then called Bill to let him know his appointment had arrived.

Elizabeth could tell several things when she sat down to talk to Bill:

- While an anecdotal survey, on her way back to Bill's office she saw no one who might be a female manager.
- In the lobby area, with its antiquated furniture and showcases, she didn't see a single picture of a woman amongst many photos of men posing with new products, new management initiatives, company collateral, etc.
- Everything told her she had just stepped into another time-warped company that would not or could not acknowledge the contributions a woman could make. Maybe she was just being hyper-vigilant, but she doubted it.

- Elizabeth knew these hiring pratices were illegal. She also found it incredibly interesting that there had to be laws created to encourage corporations to hire talented women like herself. She knew that proving discrimination of this sort was virtually impossible, but she realized this would not be a healthy environment for her, or any other talented person, to work in.

Elizabeth was surprised when her proxy interviewer let her know right away this was going to be a courtesy interview. He said to her, "While we have not already filled this position, we have an internal candidate who is most likely going to get the job. I understand you're currently with Carter Fluid Power." She was upset because she had obviously wasted her time and compromised her current job by even coming to this interview. Why had they agreed to see her in the first place?

When Elizabeth returned to work she found a note on her desk that said she needed to call Mr. Kaperson as soon as possible. Elizabeth got the vibe that something was up and that it was not good. She called Mr. Kaperson and he asked her to come to his office. When she arrived, he immediately asked her to close the door behind her. Uh-oh. He started by saying, "Well, I hear you've been talking with our friends at Enterprise

Comatose Management

Fluid Power Products. We have no problem with your interviewing with companies outside of Carter. However, we would have expected someone of your management caliber to let us know you were doing that. I am especially hurt that after offering you a tremendous promotion within Carter and a substantial pay increase, you would do this to the Carter family. You give us no choice but to let you go at this time. I feel like I am losing a daughter."

Then something unexpected happened to Elizabeth. She felt a great sense of relief. Obviously this company was never going to fully use her skills or the skills of any other woman for that matter. She could stay for another five years and the best she could probably hope for would be a promotion from lead to supervisor with another stellar 3.25% raise. She was going to have to - was being forced to - let go of the trapeze handle and grab on to the next which might provide her many more opportunities.

Mr. Kaperson went on to say, "I'm very good friends with Stephen Deen at Enterprise and he let me know you had contacted him for an interview. The sad part is that Stephen had already all but offered the job to one of their current employees by the time you contacted him. The guy getting the position is a man who goes hunting with us

Only a Man Can Manage

on a regular basis. I don't normally like to give career advice at a time like this, but the best career move for you at this point might be to take up hunting or fishing. It would allow you to network more."

Elizabeth could not believe he was actually saying these things. She had been sabotaged by "you-gotta-be-a-man-to-manage." Was he serious about her taking up hunting or fishing? Or was he just taking a parting shot? It was hard for her to accept it, but at that moment, she knew she had not realized a good return on her investment for her five years of work at Carter and that Mr. Kaperson was not a very smart man. If Mr. Kaperson had been a woman, he would most assuredly have been some kind of clerical supervisor at best.

While in college, one of Elizabeth's favorite teachers used to remind her of all the great books, poems, paintings and music no one ever heard or saw because these works did not have someone to speak for them and promote them. The brilliant creators of these works were not in a situation to promote their efforts. The creators were poor, uneducated by the world's standards, ugly, etc. and, as a result, whatever they created was destined to be silent. On the other hand, Elizabeth often thought of the mediocre to poor creations in the

Comatose Management

art world that were widely known simply because they had a channel of promotion. This poor quality, yet very well known art, was oftentimes famous simply because it was created by celebrities of one kind or another.

How often, she thought, has this happened in the business world? The truth of this was almost too difficult for her to accept. It was hard to understand that one's CEO might be grossly incompetent, but because he was in the right place at the right time, he got the job. The truth is that if someone is tall, attractive, male and has good verbal skills, he has already taken a big step toward the CEO's office.

What is the answer to this dilemma? It appears that organizations make hiring and promotion decisions on physical attributes and one's gender, just like the animal kingdom. This makes sense for the animal kingdom, but not for corporate America. We are not selecting people to mate with (well, normally) in business. We should be selecting primarily on intellectual prowess, job knowledge and experience.

Elizabeth realized that, sadly, everyone loses in this formula. Carter lost a valuable contributor who could have been a great member of the management team and Elizabeth did not maximize five years of career growth. The most important thing after all the dust had settled was that the "you-gotta-be-a-man-to-manage" mindset had been preserved at Carter and at Enterprise. The very people who should be able to see the lost opportunities will be this business killer's greatest enforcers. They find comfort and elitism within its walls. Who are these people? They are the good old boys themselves, too ignorant to see the little box they have built. Not using a significant and available resource will always harm a company in the long run, especially a resource that is leveraged as highly as management.

Elizabeth took what she had learned at Carter Fluid Power and found a customer service manager position at a medium-sized manufacturer. The company was growing at an average of 22% per year. She liked that. She was not accustomed to that kind of environment. She found her boss to be overly demanding, hard-nosed, clever and brilliant. Elizabeth knew she was going to learn a lot from her.

"Zack, give your new boss a chance to reveal her qualifications and build a strong team so you can all be successful. See her as an experienced mentor."

6

MANAGEMENT BY EMOTION

⌘ ⌘ ⌘

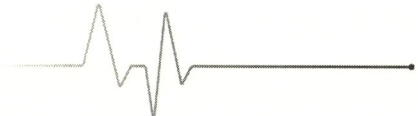

I have to admit that I love cigars. Unfortunately, I have never found a Starbucks that allows you to smoke them *in* the store. They are generous enough to let you smoke them at the tables just outside the doors, but this does not work too well when it's 37 degrees at 10:30 on a Saturday morning. Deprived of my favorite cigar, I sat down with Zack, intent on discussing the business school of hard knocks in the warmth of our favorite Starbucks. Zack and I had talked about our formal educations, but I wanted to talk with him about a degree he had probably never heard of before. I asked Zack if he had ever heard of an MBA degree. He replied, "Yes, of course." I then asked him if he had ever heard of an MBE degree. He

Comatose Management

had not heard of that degree but started guessing. "Master of Business Executives. Master of Business Engineering. Master of Business Education. Am I getting close?" I told him that he was not even warm. No, the MBE I was thinking of was the Management by Emotion degree, of which I was an expert through observation. I had observed someone in management for many years who was the polar opposite of Mr. Spock in that he never let logic get in his way. He was the poster child for the MBE degree and represented a segment of management that is more prevalent than most of us want to admit.

"The following story will provide all the information you'll ever need regarding the MBE degree. In fact, Zack, by the time I'm done you'll have earned three college credits for finishing my MBE Basics course that starts right now."

Jared had been an account manager for Gatton Material Handling Equipment Company for seven years when he was promoted to Regional Sales Manager. This meant his responsibilities went from managing and growing a territory of 65 customers to managing eight account managers. Jared was excited to get his first promotion and surprised at how large his base salary was going to be in his new position. He had been making a $47,500 base and was

Management by Emotion

averaging an additional $20,000 or so per year in commissions as an account manager. His Regional Sales Manager package included an $80,000 base with the potential of earning $45,500 per year in overrides if his sales team hit its sales budget. The National Sales Director, Mitch Gatton, explained to him that he would no longer have direct account responsibilities but would simply be managing eight account managers. He said, "The more they sell the more you make!" Jared liked the sound of money in his piggybank and Mitch knew that.

Gatton Material Handling Equipment was a fifty-year-old company that employed about 140 people. It was hard to know exactly how many employees they had because it seemed everyone in management had a different idea as to what the actual employee count was. Mitch Gatton always had the highest number, "We're almost at 200 employees now and things are going to change because we have gotten so large."

Mitch reported to his mother who owned the company. His father, the President, had died almost five years ago, leaving his mother in charge. The fact was, Mitch ran the company. His mother was seldom there. Mitch made it very clear to everyone that, "My mother has the title, but I have the job." This was supposed to indicate to everyone that he was the captain of the ship. He was the de facto President.

Jared figured out the corporate culture at Gatton early in his career there. It was really quite simple. In short it was: We will overpay you if you will put up with the demeaning work atmosphere Mitch has created. Once Mitch's dad died, it seemed like Mitch went crazy with a need for power. Mitch had never had another job in his life and it was unlikely anyone would ever hire him. He was born without his left hand and this physical handicap seemed to color everything in his life. "I can literally do more with one hand than anyone at Gatton can do with both of their hands," he would frequently say.

While it seemed that no one was particularly happy working for Mitch, he did pay well. When Mitch's mom made her infrequent visits, it seemed she was oblivious to anything going on at Gatton. She really was a figurehead in the purest sense. She thought that little Mitch, with his one hand, was God's gift to her, all the employees at Gatton, corporate America in general and mother earth.

It was Jared's second week in his new position as Regional Sales Manager when Mitch called him into his office. As Jared was entering the office

Management by Emotion

Mitch asked him to close the office door behind him. Jared instantly assumed he had already done something wrong and was in trouble. Mitch asked Jared to sit down and get comfortable. Mitch sat at his desk and just stared at Jared for about thirty seconds, which seems like an eternity in situations like that. "I have an assignment for you, Jared, which is one of the most important in the company." This made Jared sit up. "I want you to go to our Des Moines location and replace the account manager who just quit...I mean that we fired! What a worthless piece of humanity he was. God's good oxygen was wasted on him every time he breathed. Get with Debra in HR and run an ad for his replacement in the newspaper as soon as you leave my office."

Jared asked. "Mitch, do we not use any of the Internet job search sites such as Hot Jobs or Monster? It seems like that would be much more cost effective with a broader reach."

With a look on his face that Jared had never noticed before, Mitch said to Jared, "Don't question the business wisdom of the person who is running this company. We've always run ads in newspapers and it works best. You would do well to listen to my leadership for now and not challenge things. Now get with Debra and get the

Comatose Management

ball rolling. I'm looking forward to the quality applicants you will bring back to the home office for second interviews."

Jared's head was swimming when he left Mitch's office. What just happened? Was he disrespectful to Mitch? Had he done something inappropriate? He was scared and confused. He had a wife and a three-year-old child at home. He did not need to ruin his career with a bad interaction with the boss. Jared sat down at his cubicle and didn't realize Mitch had followed him. "One last thing Jared. Never, ever, hire anyone named William or Randy. We've never had any luck with account managers who have those names. Don't even waste your time doing first interviews with them."

All Jared could say in return was, "Yes sir." He thought, what's wrong with people named William and Randy?

Jared dutifully got with Debra, who took care of all the travel arrangements for the Regional Sales Managers in addition to her regular HR duties. Debra was an old-fashioned "Girl Friday" who did a little of everything for the sales department and HR. She was attractive and had a nice personality although a little chubby by some people's standards. There had been rumors that Debra and Mitch had an affair several years ago. Most of the office believed it was true because he was a

Management by Emotion

little too familiar with Debra in his dealings with her. It was not uncommon for Mitch to be talking with her and have his arm around her waist. This seemed to make everyone uncomfortable except for the two of them. There were also times when Mitch bought Debra gifts that seemed very inappropriate, especially the time he gave her a $500 Victoria's Secret gift card and advertised what he had done to the entire office. Mitch was married, but this fact never seemed to get in the way of his flirtatious behavior with Debra.

Per Mitch's instructions, Jared asked Debra, "I need to go to Des Moines to do some interviewing. Can you take care of putting an ad in the newspaper and arranging my flight and hotel?"

"Sure, I'll be happy to help you. I do at least one of these each week so I've gotten it down to a science."

After providing Debra with additional details, Jared walked back to his cubicle. He looked over his shoulder to make sure no one was following him this time, namely Mitch. He sat down at his desk and grabbed his calculator. He thought to himself, this company has about 140 employees and about 80 of them are account managers. If Debra has to arrange to replace more than one every week, that means we have about a 60% turnover in the sales team. For their industry, an

Comatose Management

average turnover rate in the sales team should have been closer to 20%. More than half of Gatton Material Handling Equipment's sales force leaves for greener pastures every year. How could that be happening, he thought? Something is wrong when the sales turnover is that high. Jared had frequently heard departing account managers say Gatton was a crazy house and they could not take it anymore. What did they mean when they said things like "crazy house?" They would also make comments about how nothing seemed to be predictable with Mitch. One day you would be his best friend and the next day you were his worst enemy. Jared had just experienced that with Mitch when he became hostile after Jared made the mistake of recommending the Internet job search sites. Behavior like that from Mitch certainly didn't make Jared feel more secure in his job and it most likely had a similar effect on other employees.

As time passed, Jared was starting to learn the ropes of management and was beginning to feel more comfortable about most everything. He had learned to avoid Mitch for one thing. He had figured that out on his own, for the most part, but several of his peers had advised him to do the same if he wanted to keep his sanity. Jared thought it odd that the leader of a company was

Management by Emotion

actively being ostracized by his own employees. The very communications that should have been the strongest were intentionally being minimized by some of Mitch's direct reports. Jared decided to take the high road and put all of these negative thoughts behind him. He was about to get on a jet and start interviewing in Des Moines to replace the account manager who had been terminated. The account manager may have actually quit, but Jared was going to believe what Mitch told him – he had been fired.

In preparation for the journey, Jared decided to look at the records of the ex-Des Moines account manager and realized he had not been fired. He was among the top 20% of all account managers at Gatton. He had quit. Mitch had lied.

It was Monday morning at 5:00 a.m. and Jared was boarding his flight for Des Moines. Mitch always required that the Regional Sales Managers be at their destination city at 8:00 a.m. With time zone changes, this required some very early flights sometimes. He also required that they not leave the destination city to return home until after 5:00 p.m. This made for some long workdays and workweeks. The irony of all this was that Mitch worked about 20 to 25 hours per week and never traveled to any of the remote locations. This double standard really bothered some employees

Comatose Management

in the office, especially those who traveled a lot. Jared always felt that if he was treated fairly then it did not matter what the boss did.

Just as Jared was crossing the threshold into the plane his cell phone rang. While balancing his attaché and carry-on, he managed to see who was calling. It was Mitch. By some acrobatic ability, he was able to answer the phone. As soon as Jared answered Mitch said, "I thought you and I were going to review the Des Moines territory before you left to start interviewing."

Jared replied, "I don't recall any conversation like that, but I would have been happy to do that with you. I'll be glad to send you my analysis by email when I get to the hotel."

"Well Jared, I'm just not happy with that solution. I always sit down with my Regional Sales Managers before they start interviewing replacements. How many applicants do you have set up to interview?"

"I think I have twelve applicants to interview this week."

Mitch snapped back, "That's it? Did you use any other ways to find applicants other than the newspaper?"

Jared was stunned at this point and hardly knew how to respond. "You told me in your office that you didn't want to use any internet job search sites."

"Jared, for God's sake, that doesn't mean you can't use other things on the internet like sales discussion forums or web sites that list jobs just in our industry."

"But Mitch, I took your comments to mean that we should only use the newspaper and Debra never mentioned anything else to me."

"Well Jared, we'll just write this one off as a rookie mistake and you'll have a chance to improve next time. Hope you find someone who will do a better job than that loser we just fired. Have a good trip."

"I'll do my best Mitch. Would you like me to send you the analysis I've already done on the territory?"

"That won't be necessary. I'll see it when you get back. Good-bye." And with that, Mitch hung up the phone. Jared was confused. Did he miss something in Mitch's office that day when they were talking about this venture? Did Mitch forget what he had told Jared? Was Mitch intentionally creating a win-lose situation for himself and Jared? No matter what move Jared made, it looked like Mitch was going to change the rules to trip him up.

Comatose Management

After landing in Des Moines, Jared took a taxi to his hotel where he was going to interview the candidates. His first interview was in the early afternoon so he had some time to relax a little and grab something to eat at the hotel. Just as he was about to head down to the restaurant, he got another call on his cell phone from Mitch. Mitch seemed much more under control and almost contrite at this point. Mitch started out by saying, "Did your plane trip go okay?"

Jared immediately sensed he was being disingenuous. "Yes it was fine, Mitch. How can I help you?"

"Well, I think your promotion has created a problem for us. My mom reminded me today when she was visiting that she doesn't want any employees promoted without her approval."

There was a note of panic in Mitch's voice. "Did you talk with her about your promotion prior to being promoted?"

Jared was shocked; of course he had not talked with her about his promotion. Mitch came to him with the idea. "No Mitch, I have never said anything to your mom about my promotion *before* I was promoted or *afterwards*."

"Well, that's too bad because now I'll have to handle the situation. Here's what I need you to do. Don't say anything to Mom about your promotion and if she asks if you've been promoted say something like, 'Well, Mitch has said that my request for promotion is being considered but he needs to talk to you first.' I'll make sure that she doesn't see any written material about the promotion before I have a chance to talk to her. I'll get with her and tell her about the promotion you want and I'm sure she'll be just fine with it and then we can carry on as usual. But, for now, just stay under the radar with her. I'll get this fixed and you're going to owe me for this one."

Jared was mad. Mitch had bungled his promotion by overstepping his boundaries and not checking with mommy first. Mitch had positioned it so it appeared that all of this was Jared's fault. Furthermore, he wanted Jared to lie to his mom about the entire ordeal to cover Mitch's manipulative ways. And, unbelievably, he was creating the cover-up in order to deceive his own *mother*. Mitch's mother was uninvolved with the business and seemed indifferent as to how Mitch was managing things. This cover-up was not even necessary in Jared's estimation.

Jared was beginning to feel like Mitch was throwing one obstacle after another in his way. He was lobbing things at him that Jared couldn't really control. Was Mitch in Jared's corner? Was he in *any* of the employees' corner? Did Mitch feel threatened by his own limitations? Did he feel he needed to prove something because everyone knew he worked for his mother? Did his mother over indulge him when he was younger, making him feel he was above common rules of decency?

Most likely Mitch had no perspective on anything outside of Gatton because he had never worked anywhere else and was spoiled as a kid. There was no objectivity. There was no other life or business experience. Mitch had created his own benchmarks in an unhealthy circular way. As a result, the de facto CEO of the Gatton Material Handling Equipment Company was operating almost purely by emotion and feelings rather than using experience or logic to make sound decisions.

Jared was beginning to wonder if he was ever going to be able to actually start interviewing candidates he had carefully picked, albeit from newspaper ads only. He had vowed that the next time Mitch called he was going to ignore the call, at least for a while, in order to give himself a little break from Mitch. He was going to discretely ask the other Regional Sales Managers when he got back to the office if they had been experiencing this same kind of irrational behavior from Mitch. Maybe it was something Mitch did to all the new Regional Sales Managers as kind of a Mitch boot camp of sorts.

Management by Emotion

  His first candidate was nothing short of a complete disaster. He came in wearing a baseball cap and blue jeans. Jared understood Gatton was an industrial distributor, but for an applicant to come dressed like that for an interview seemed a little over the top. Clearly, he was going to take a pass on this individual and was going to conduct a short courtesy interview. His second and third candidates later that day at least dressed appropriately but were about as skilled in sales as Jared's cat. Finally, at 9:00 a.m. on his second day of interviewing he found a good candidate. He was a nice looking person who had 15 years of material handling equipment experience and seemed to talk the sales game quite admirably. Thirty minutes into this interview Jared's cell phone rang. The caller ID indicated that it was a call from Mitch. Time seemed to almost freeze at this point for Jared. Was this going to be a call from Mitch steering him in another unexpected direction? He decided not to answer the phone and let it go to voice mail. Why should he interrupt an interview with one of his most promising candidates in order to have another bizarre conversation with Mitch? He would call him back. It made Jared feel more powerful by ignoring Mitch. The interview ended about 20 minutes after Mitch's call and Jared thanked the candidate for coming by. He assured the interviewee he would be getting back in touch with him.

As soon as the candidate left the room, Jared returned Mitch's call. Mitch wanted to know how things were going with the interviews. Jared was happy to report he had found a candidate who seemed to be promising. Mitch asked him a few questions about the prospective employee and seemed pleased with Mitch's answers. Jared was beginning to think maybe the worst was behind him. Possibly Mitch had a bad week or was just "breaking in" Jared and the emotional behavior was going to stop. Mitch asked, "What is the name of this candidate?"

Jared was holding the applicant's employment application and looked at it to be sure he got it correct, "Daniel Williams." There was a long silence and Jared could tell Mitch was speaking through clenched teeth when he said, "I thought I told you not to hire anyone with the name of William."

Jared responded, "His *last* name is Williams, not his first name. And I thought you said it was 'William' not 'Williams' that I was to avoid."

"Jared, you've been a Regional Sales Manager for only a short period and you have challenged my authority on several occasions already. This cannot go unaddressed. Finish your interviews in

Management by Emotion

Des Moines and we will have a closed door session when you get back."

Jared responded with, "That will be fine. I'll see you when I'm back in the office. Good bye." Then he hung up on Mitch.

He stopped caring at that moment.

Jared felt like a limp rag doll after this phone call. He realized Mitch was running on nothing but immature emotion. Logic was something foreign to Mitch. Jared knew he had previously not seen this very large deficiency in Mitch because he had been an account manager and was never in the office. Jared's Regional Sales Manager had obviously done an admirable job of insulating him from the reckless behavior of Mitch. Every time Jared had a conversation with Mitch, it was if he was talking to a young child having a temper tantrum. Logic, strategy and experience played no role in Mitch's little world.

Jared quickly figured he was no longer in the mood to interview any further candidates. Mitch's out of control emotional outbursts had made effective interviewing impossible. When it comes to interviewing, the interviewer has to sell the interviewee and Jared was in no mood for selling Gatton at that moment. He picked up the phone and canceled the other eight interviews he had set up for the next two days. He knew he could just tell Mitch and Debra that none of the other candidates were worth looking at. Jared needed a little time to sort things out before heading back. Trying to convince people to take a job working for a company run by someone like Mitch was not on his agenda right now.

When Jared returned to the office two days later he passed Mitch in the reception area. Frankly, by this time Jared wanted to tear the little one-handed idiot's head off but instead greeted him warmly. Surprisingly, Mitch responded in like kind. It was as if everything was fine and Jared was the most important person at Gatton Material Handling Equipment Company. Once back at his desk he noticed an email from Debra that read in part, "Mitch would like to go ahead and bring Daniel Williams in for a second interview and wanted to know if you were able to find any other good candidates. Would you please send me the paperwork for Mr. Williams?" What? Had Mitch changed his psychiatric medications since he had last talked with him on the phone? It was as if things at Gatton were suddenly normal again. Jared was afraid to let himself get too excited.

He took Daniel Williams' paperwork over to Debra's desk in response to her email. As he laid the paperwork down he asked, "How are things

Management by Emotion

in the office since I've been gone? What kind of mood is Mitch in?"

Debra responded, "Nothing really has happened since you left and Mitch has been in a great mood of course." Jared thought for a second and wondered what the "of course" meant at the end of her response. He could not resist asking.

"What do you mean by, 'of course'?"

Debra just blurted out, "Yesterday Mitch went back to getting counseling again. It is hell around here when he is not seeing his shrink at least once or twice a week. When he goes to counseling things aren't too bad around here. Then he stops and we get the old drama queen, Mitch, back again. By the way, I'm not telling you anything he doesn't talk about freely in the office. Mitch thinks it's cool to go to a shrink just as all the Hollywood celebrities do. Well, let me tell you we are more than happy to have him go."

Jared stepped out on the ice a little further and asked, "Does Mitch have some kind of psychiatric disorder like schizophrenia or is he bi-polar?"

Debra laughed, "We don't think so. We just think he is a drama queen. Honestly, just between you and me, his mother gave him so much preferential treatment when he was growing up because of his missing hand that he has a very small grip on reality – mentally *and* physically.

Comatose Management

That is all there is to it in our opinion. The fact that he has never had another job doesn't help too much either."

Jared didn't know what else to say other than, "Thanks for the update" and went back to his desk.

Later that day Mitch called Jared into his office. Jared was not afraid of being reprimanded by Mitch for two reasons: 1. Mitch had started his counseling again, 2. Jared had decided he was either going to quit his Regional Sales Manager job and go back to his account manager position at Gatton or leave altogether if Mitch had another one of his uncontrolled emotional outbursts.

Mitch instructed Jared to close the door behind him and have a seat just as he had done before. Apparently this was a ritual of his. At almost whispered levels he asked Jared, "What do you think of Debra? Should I get rid of her? She really isn't that great looking and has an attitude sometimes. My mom thinks I should replace her with someone who is nicer and more respectful to me and everyone else. What do you think?"

Sometimes we have moments in our lives when we tell the pure truth and it is good for our souls. It feels good too. This was one of those moments for Jared.

"Mitch, you'd be crazy to get rid of Debra. She's been here for years, knows the system and from what I can observe she is quite respectful of you. You shouldn't be concerned about how *nice* she is or her personal appearance. Can she do the job and does she get along with everyone? The answer to both of those questions is yes."

Sometimes when logic hits careless, destructive and immature behavior in the head it responds in a positive way. Somewhere deep in the depths of Mitch's cerebellum there was a seed of logic that was struggling to grow. "You know, you're right, Jared. What was I thinking? Thanks for giving me your input and I look forward to interviewing your applicant. Debra said he is a strong candidate based on your comments and his resume."

"Speaking of your mom, where does she stand in relation to my being promoted to Regional Sales Manager? When I was in Des Moines you called and told me she was upset about not being consulted about my promotion."

Mitch looked down at the floor for a second and said, "Oh, I had forgotten all about that. You should know by now about my mom. She should have been a dramatic actor. Up one second and down the next. She is your comrade today and your enemy tomorrow. Her low emotional quotient drives me crazy sometimes. This whole organization should be happy I am here to insulate everyone from her irrational behavior.

Comatose Management

Don't worry about this issue anymore. She hasn't brought it up in days and that means it wasn't all that important to her in the first place."

Jared responded, "Well, I'm glad it didn't turn out to be a problem." Jared asked Mitch if there were any other issues that needed to be discussed and Mitch indicated in the negative. Jared quickly exited Mitch's office and went back to his cubicle to consider what had transpired over the last few weeks.

Jared had now observed two different Mitches as de facto President at Gatton in his last seven years with the company. The Mitch who managed him from a distance was a leader who seemed reasonable although not necessarily brilliant or experienced. Recently he had observed Mitch as his direct boss. This was the out of control person who treated Jared completely differently as a direct report. Why did he not believe the stories about Mitch's irrational behavior all those years when he had heard the rumors? Could Mitch have an issue of control? Mitch's inability to control his emotions was obviously a contributor to his outbursts.

People are desperate for leadership at work. They are looking for a leader they can trust, who cares about them and is consistent. Mitch has none of those qualities because he has not learned

Management by Emotion

to control his emotions. He *reacts* to every situation instead of *responding*. The employees have no respect for him. Mitch's direct reports at Gatton Material Handling Equipment Company come to work every day not knowing what kind of leader they will have for the day. When that happens, people protect themselves by being numb at work. They turn off their brains and their motivation.

The greatest irony of all this is that companies with leaders like this have to pay higher salaries to get people to stay. In other words, they are literally paying more for less. Over time, all of the employees will be replaced with indifferent zombies going through the motions. And the final paradox is that the Mitches of the world *like* having zombies on the payroll; they're easier to control.

About the Author

Scott R. Sheaffer, CSE, DTM, publishes Sales Tips Blog by Scott R. Sheaffer (salestipsbyscott.com) and is a contributing writer for other national publications. He lives in Dallas, Texas and has worked in sales, sales management and sales training for over 20 years in companies ranging from small enterprises to Fortune 500 companies. The focus of Scott's industry experience has been with industrial distributors. He is a graduate of Baylor University and a member of ASTD.

Sales Tips Blog by Scott R. Sheaffer

Scott publishes a twice-weekly blog post on issues faced by sales professionals and sales management. You can receive these short and informative posts at no charge by email or RSS feed. Go to salestipsbyscott.com for more information.

You can follow Scott on social media by visiting salestipsbyscott.com/about.

Made in the USA